MEDITATION

for

MULTITASKERS

YOUR GUIDE TO FINDING PEACE BETWEEN THE PINGS

DAVID DILLARD-WRIGHT, PhD

Aadamsmedia
Avon, Massachusetts

For Jessica

Published by
Adams Media, a division of F+W Media, Inc.
57 Littlefield Street, Avon, MA 02322. U.S.A.
www.adamsmedia.com

ISBN 10: 1-4405-2490-4
ISBN 13: 978-1-4405-2490-5
eISBN 10: 1-4405-2671-0
eISBN 13: 978-1-4405-2671-8

Printed in the United States of America.

10   9   8   7   6   5   4   3   2   1

Library of Congress Cataloging-in-Publication Data
Dillard-Wright, David
Meditation for multitaskers with cd / David Dillard-Wright.
p. cm.
ISBN 978-1-4405-2490-5
1. Meditation. 2. Human multitasking. I. Title.
BF637.M4D55 2011
158.1'2—dc22
2011010371

This book is intended as general information only, and should not be used to diagnose or treat any health condition. In light of the complex, individual, and specific nature of health problems, this book is not intended to replace professional medical advice. The ideas, procedures, and suggestions in this book are intended to supplement, not replace, the advice of a trained medical professional. Consult your physician before adopting any of the suggestions in this book, as well as about any condition that may require diagnosis or medical attention. The author and publisher disclaim any liability arising directly or indirectly from the use of this book.

Many of the designations used by manufacturers and sellers to distinguish their product are claimed as trademarks. Where those designations appear in this book and Adams Media was aware of a trademark claim, the designations have been printed with initial capital letters.

CD performed by Jim Infantino, Dan Cantor, and Lorena Perez,
and produced by Notable Productions.

This book is available at quantity discounts for bulk purchases.
For information, please call 1-800-289-0963.

CONTENTS

ACKNOWLEDGMENTS

Dr. Ravinder Jerath taught me how pranayama works within the context of human physiology. I am grateful for his many conversations and illustrations. Thanks to Victoria Sandbrook, Jennifer Lawler, and everyone at Adams Media for giving me this project and bringing it to completion. Thanks to all the devas, saints, and sages for giving me the inspiration to teach and write.

INTRODUCTION:
MEDITATION AND THE MULTITASKER

Feeling stressed out and too busy to take a breather? That's no surprise, considering the pace of daily life. Those technologies that were supposed to make our lives easier? Nope. They add ever more demands on us.

Does it sometimes feel you have no time for conversation, no time for cooking a meal, no time for hobbies or exercise? No time for, well, life?

If you want to unplug, get off the treadmill, and make life a little more humane, you're facing a bit of a battle, because wanting to live well means going against the tide of society, which seems bent on making us either produce or consume twenty-four hours a day.

We live in a world of continual movement, of a mad dash for more. The Hindu tradition calls it the *Kali Yuga*, the dark age, a time when technology improves but moral standards decline, a time of darkness, ignorance, and suffering. The Kali Yuga is a time when it is hard to be good, when the whole society seems bent on corruption and greed. But the Kali Yuga isn't inevitable: It's more a state of mind than a destiny set in stone. To change things, we just need a new way of thinking.

Meditation is that new way of thinking. That may sound floaty and, well, "New Agey," to a practical-minded person like yourself.

If you're a multitasker, you're more concerned with getting things done than with creating peace. But that's exactly the sort of either/or thinking that this book challenges.

What if you didn't have to choose between being active and productive and being calm and centered? What if there were a way to make the two go together?

Here you'll learn how to be more productive while at the same time starting a meditation practice. You won't have to run away to a Himalayan ashram or fast for days on end or walk on hot coals: This book uses the time that you otherwise would have wasted and turns it into an opportunity for positive thinking and personal growth. Because multitasking is both stressful and inefficient, gradually moving to doing only one thing at a time will make you more focused and energetic. You will learn to discipline your mind and unlock your creative potential through meditation.

Even if you have as little as one minute to spare, you will find ways to get started on a calmer path. You will learn how to make your home and work space more tranquil, how to make any task easier, and how to cut through obstacles in any endeavor. You'll have more energy and more free time. You'll find yourself enjoying life more and smiling for no reason. Your secret will be so simple that no one would believe you if you told them.

Deep breathing and concentration: It seems impossible that a practice so simple could bring such strong results, but it's true! Even in the short term, you will experience a better quality of life almost immediately from the practice of meditation. You will feel better emotionally and physically, feel less at the mercy of your circumstances, and find solutions to problems like never before. You will live with greater enthusiasm and energy, and your responsibilities will seem lighter. People will wonder if you have started taking a new prescription or met someone new, when in fact you have just uncovered the natural happiness available to everyone.

Each chapter in this book explains a particular aspect of meditation and offers tips and exercises to put the principles into practice, along with inspiring quotes. You will move from practicing meditation one-to-five minutes at a time to practicing fifteen-to-twenty minutes twice a day.

In addition to the timed meditation exercises, you'll also find solar exercises and lunar exercises. The solar exercises are geared toward rational thought and strategic planning, while the lunar exercises focus on creativity and intuition. You will need to use both of these dimensions of yourself in the practice of meditation, for while you may lean one way or another, we all have active and receptive parts of ourselves. Meditation is about approaching reality with your whole self, and completing these exercises fine-tunes your personality and intellect so that you develop one-pointed awareness. Rationality can be harnessed to serve the process of meditation, and intuition can be strengthened to increase insight. When rationality and intuition work together, self-realization happens.

As a multitasker, you're committed to productivity, but your fragmented approach is more harmful than helpful. By learning how to focus on one task at a time, and using meditation to train your mind and center yourself, you will become a productive, less stressed person.

Sound like a plan? Let's get started!

How to Use the CD

The audio CD that accompanies this book is meant to help you meditate no matter how little time you have. It includes several guided meditations as short as one minute, plus others that are five, ten, and even twenty minutes long. Use this CD at any time for a refreshing meditation break—even if you're sitting at your desk!

PART I

YOUR ATTENTION, PLEASE!

CHAPTER 1

COSTS OF MULTITASKING
AND MEDITATION'S ANSWERS

You answer phone calls and e-mails simultaneously. When your kids have questions about their homework, you don't stop cooking dinner to answer. When you get on that weekly conference call, you continue writing your report rather than wait half an hour to finish it. You may fight the urge to reply to a text while you drive, but when the phone rings, your Bluetooth earpiece picks up automatically. You even watch television at dinnertime. Congratulations! You're getting a lot accomplished.

Or are you? Before you give yourself a pat on the back, read this chapter. The consequences of multitasking will shock you.

How much multitasking do you do every day? This quiz should help you assess times when you tend to focus on more than one thing at a time. Count how many of the following statements sound like you:

Are You a Multitasker?

Reading

1. When I read, I usually have music playing in the background.
2. When I read, I often have the television on in the background.
3. I read online news more often than I read print books.
4. I keep multiple tabs open when I'm browsing/reading online.
5. I won't read news articles longer than one page online.
6. I often start a book before I've finished the one I was already reading, though I usually finish both.
7. I rarely finish reading books.

Meals

1. I usually have music playing during meals.
2. I usually have the television on during meals.
3. I have taken important phone calls during meals.
4. I have taken important e-mails on my smartphone during meals.

Commuting

1. I have answered my cell phone while driving.
2. I have texted or e-mailed while driving.
3. I listen to music while driving.
4. I have conversations with my passengers while driving.

5. I respond to work e-mails during my commute.
6. I use voice recognition and text-to-speech programs to read and write text messages while I'm driving.

Work

1. I continue typing while I'm on the phone.
2. I check and/or answer e-mails during meetings.
3. I check and/or answer e-mails while someone else is in my office or cubicle.
4. I use an instant messaging service at the office.
5. I use social media at the office.
6. I stream television shows or movies on my computer and listen or watch while I work.
7. I listen to music while I work.
8. I have a job that requires me to be on call.
9. I take work home.

Non-Office Work

1. I move to the next customer before finishing with the one before.
2. I work on different projects at the same time, without grouping them into sections or phases.
3. I prefer to work spontaneously rather than structuring my time.
4. I have been called "flighty" or "unreliable."

5. I mix work materials with personal materials.
6. I use my down time at work to catch up on personal matters.

For College and Graduate Students

1. I text or surf the Internet during class.
2. I study while watching television or listening to music.
3. I always keep tabs on my social media pages.
4. I prefer to work on two or three assignments at the same time.
5. I maintain my social life even during midterms and finals.
6. I often complete major projects by staying up all night.
7. I take incompletes or withdraw from classes to avoid failing them.

For Stay-at-Home Parents

1. I talk on the phone while at the grocery store.
2. I fold laundry while watching television.
3. I read or listen to the radio while eating with the kids.
4. I don't keep a weekly schedule of chores; I just do things when they need doing.
5. I feel like I always have to answer the phone.
6. I don't miss having time to myself.

Telephone

1. I answer my phone every time it rings.
2. My phone rings or vibrates regardless of the hour or where I am.
3. My phone alerts me to work e-mails while I'm at home.
4. My phone alerts me to work e-mails while I'm at work.
5. My phone alerts me to personal e-mails while I'm at home.
6. My phone alerts me to personal e-mails while I'm at work.
7. I always answer text messages quickly.

Results

If you said "yes" to 0–8 questions, you tend to focus on what you're doing, but a second priority can still sneak up on you and wreak havoc.

If you said "yes" to 9–16 questions, you tend to multitask. Your multitasking habits are leaving you little time to breathe. Start making changes now and you'll reclaim your much needed me-time.

If you said "yes" to 17–24 questions, you are a diehard multitasker. Your time may be well-managed and you may get more done than the people around you, but you may be surprised to find that the root of your success is stressing you out more than the things you can't get to. If you're going to beat multitasking before it beats you, you'll need to make big changes now!

If you said "yes" to more than 25 questions, you are multitasking way too much! You're the person who lives twenty-five hour days and thinks by minutes, not hours. You'll only be able to reclaim yourself if you start working meditation into that airtight routine of yours.

Birth of the Multitasker

Humans have always been multitaskers. Our ancestors kept an eye out for saber-toothed tigers while they prepared the evening meal. They kept the baby from toddling off the cliff while they washed clothes in the river.

But humans have reached a point where the pressure to multitask (and the pressure *of* multitasking) has outstripped the brain's ability to keep pace. Today, multitasking jeopardizes the very productivity that it was meant to safeguard.

While multitasking itself may be as old as the human species, the term wasn't used in its present sense until the 1990s, when it made its way over from computer science, and became a resume skill set for the first time. The possibilities seemed limitless: checking e-mail on the daily commute! Doing office work on the beach! The trouble was that no one bothered to think about how all of this newfound "efficiency" would impact the psychological and mental states of workers. Much less did anyone think that the claims of increased productivity should actually be tested.

The Hidden Price of Multitasking

Americans aren't handling the pressure to multitask as well as we'd like to think. The Society for Human Resource Management claims that 70 percent of employees let work spill over into nights and weekends—and more than half of people who did said they'd done so due to "self-imposed pressure." Americans threw away a combined total of 465 million vacation days, according to expedia.com, yet the Institute for the Future reports that 60 percent of white-collar workers are overwhelmed by their work.

Business researcher Jonathan Spira estimated, in an interview with the *New York Times*, that multitasking costs the U.S. economy alone $650 billion in decreased efficiency. Diehard multitaskers are likely to be losing 2.1 productive hours to multitasking at work every day.

The Institute of Psychiatry at the University of London found that your IQ will fall ten points when you field e-mails, texts, and phone calls the way multitaskers tend to. That means you'd be more productive if you were high on marijuana (which only causes a four-point drop).

Teenagers were more likely to give up talking on the phone and watching TV, one survey said, than give up texting and e-mailing. Texting while driving has become so prolific that statewide bans have begun to battle the increasingly lethal practice.

Diehard multitaskers are the poster children for sixty-hour work weeks, desk rage, and sleep disorders. If you're one of them, you're at high risk for the stress-related diseases that make up 80 percent of American healthcare costs. And if you haven't felt like you've run out of creative ideas, you will soon.

Recent studies have shown that our innovative spirit is dying. A researcher at Indiana University recently discovered that American creativity is objectively dwindling, and a Stanford study discovered that multitaskers are less creative and adaptive than people who focus when they learn. Russell Poldrack, a UCLA associate professor of psychology, says, "Even if you learn while multitasking, that learning is less flexible and more specialized, so you cannot retrieve the information as easily."

When your focus is interrupted by other tasks, you lose the ability to make out-of-the-box connections and recall information from your short-term memory. Research also confirms that the interruptions that perhaps began as momentary ones often spiral into long detours from important work. It often takes over twenty minutes for workers to recover from pausing to read *one* e-mail. You might also be tempted to think that some people are "good" at multitasking and others are not, or that different learning styles respond to the processing of information differently. At least one study, in the *Proceedings of the National Academy of Science*, reported that heavy multitaskers are actually less skillful at switching from task to task than their more moderate counterparts. According to the study, the lower performance by heavy multitaskers stems from an inability to filter irrelevant information; decreased attention led to poorer performance on the assigned task.

Why Doesn't Multitasking Work?

Even the simplest task requires a long series of decisions. Making toast requires decisions about how many slices, whether to have jam, and which plate to put it on (to name just a few). Your brain has to figure out the order in which to make and execute these decisions, prioritize the most important aspects of the task, and put the details in the proper order.

The complexity of a single project can cause delays as your brain makes those decisions. When multiple tasks are added into the mix (sending an e-mail from your smartphone while writing a grocery list while making the toast) the delays are compounded exponentially—

that is, if you're doing three tasks, the delays aren't three times as long; they're nine times as long—or thirty-six or seventy-two.

"We are what we repeatedly do. Excellence then,
is not an act, but a habit."

—ARISTOTLE

How Your Brain Works

The executive function of the brain does the prioritizing part of a task. But your brain accomplishes its work not by doing multiple things at once but by preferring one set of information over another. So it will pay attention to some things over other things. For example, it may prioritize visual cues over auditory cues, which means that when you're on the phone with your boss and skimming this month's budget report, you brain may be focusing on the budget report (visual cue), not your boss (auditory cue), which could have the unfortunate effect of your not hearing the new deadline she just gave you for your pet project. In other words, given too much to attend to, your brain will make mistakes.

Ever typed an e-mail while on the phone with your spouse? Your partner may have said to bring milk, bread, eggs, and soup home from the store, and you brought home milk, bread, a bag of Cheetos, and a movie. You might have meant well, but the missing attention from the conversation went into the e-mail, which probably suffered in some small way as well. Think of all these mental misfires compounded each day, all of the work done haphazardly, all of the time lost. The results of this massive distraction are overwhelming.

Brains and Computers

The fervor that created the multitasking craze began as people tried to model themselves after their machines. As the machines got better, people began to expect more from themselves as well. Remember the old dial-up Internet connections, the pings and beeps, followed by static, and at long last, the browser window gradually blinked to life?

We used to be much more conscious of the singular flow of information, and opening multiple windows would immediately be punished with crippling slowness. As maddening as dial-up could be, at least it meant doing only one thing at a time; you were either checking e-mail, or typing, or surfing the Net—but not all three at the same time.

In the sense that our brains are like computers, they're more like dial-up than broadband, at least when it comes to executing tasks. Our brains already do so much with each passing second—integrating sensory experience (taste, touch, sound, sight, and smell) with memories and imaginings, while moving the body around in the world, manipulating objects, and executing plans. Adding more to the mix results in the same crippling slowness that you remember from the dial-up days—things get done, they just don't get done quickly or well.

And unlike the computer, you feel all sorts of pressures that silicon chips don't (or at least don't yet). You have to worry about your emotional and social life as well. We are complex, social, emotional beings, which is a lot of added baggage already. We can't just check all that at the door in order to become more efficient. If we are to be efficient, we must be efficient *as ourselves*, and this means taking account of our complex natures.

Think of a particularly stressful period in your own life, when you felt a lot of time pressure. For students, this might be during final exams, or, for a business executive, right before an important presentation. When we get stressed, we often do what the experts tell us to do, which is to make a to-do list. The idea is that making a list will bring some control to the chaos and help us to see the finite nature of the work, which will, in turn, create a feeling of calm.

Did you ever notice how making a list sometimes has the exact opposite effect? You remember a thousand things that you had forgotten that you were supposed to do? The list seems like a huge beast with a thousand magically regenerating heads that will never be conquered with your puny wooden sword. The list creates panic rather than quells it. Why is that the case? Often it's because you created the list in an unfiltered manner. Your brain did not process and rank the information. In short, the executive functions weren't done.

That panic you felt when on looking at your endless list? That's exactly how the brain responds to multitasking—with panic. The brain likes a neat queue of tasks with predetermined beginnings and endings, and it will function very well under those conditions. When asked to do everything at once, it will crash like an Apple IIe running AutoCAD.

Imagine a highway during rush hour: there is simply too much traffic to move freely through the lanes. Almost anything can start a traffic jam: a cardboard box in the road, the glare of the sun in drivers' eyes, construction work, or a paving project. That small bottleneck from a lost lane or a change in speed quickly becomes a standstill stretching for miles. The traffic jam only clears when the traffic dips below the threshold that the road was designed to handle. In the same way, we can expect a kind of overheating or overcongestion when we try to do too many things at once with our minds.

The overload manifests itself in the form of the stress response, which is now a leading cause of illness, ranging from anxiety and depression to heart disease and stroke. Our bodies are not designed to live in a permanent state of emergency. But that's what we force them to do when we perpetually clutter our mental environment with too many different tasks and streams of information. A calm, clear, mental environment leads to increased productivity, better health, and improved moods.

To be sure, multitasking gives small payoffs: we feel constantly entertained and busy, which can seem satisfying. But this small payoff does not justify the very real costs of multitasking.

Why Multitasking Appeals

We probably all know that checking every e-mail that hits our inboxes is not the best way to manage time. We also know that keeping Facebook open and constantly Googling everything probably will lead to a lack of productivity. So why do we do it? On one level, we fear being automatons, mindless processors of work. We love distraction because it reminds us that we have a life outside our responsibilities. It's also a way to avoid the decision-making process of prioritizing tasks and solving problems. The occasional amusing YouTube video or personal e-mail is just enough of a jolt to keep us coming back for more. So we flit from one distraction to another, hoping that one of them will yield the illusive satisfaction that we crave.

Monotasking Hint

When working on a computer-based project, close all computer windows that do not directly pertain to that project. Consider using a computer that does not have a connection to the Internet or complete all Internet-related research ahead of time. Try occasionally using a pen and a sheet of paper as a reminder of what it's like to reflect without interruption.

Stress and the Human Mind

A little loss of time or efficiency doesn't sound that bad, though, right? If it were just a matter of wasting time, multitasking wouldn't be the worst thing in the world. However, many studies have shown greater levels of stress and anxiety in individuals who routinely multitask. In other words, far from a kind of benign susceptibility to online amusement, multitasking causes people to lead less satisfactory and less healthy lives.

A recent survey found that people in industrialized nations are in fact less happy and content than folks in less-developed countries. It's no wonder that 62 percent of Americans say that work has a significant impact on the stress in their lives: The human nervous system will never get an upgrade. There are physical limits to how many things you can do at once. More work means more stress. And stress, in turn, has a significant impact on the quality of your life.

Your brain needs downtime the same way your body needs sleep. Researchers now believe that this time doing "nothing" is very important for your brain to process information and experiences and forge new creative connections.

Think about your own life. Don't you often have your best ideas in the shower? The brain needs downtime—indeed, needs *boredom*—in order to rest and recover and to process new information. While jumping from task to task may feel productive, it's not. From a neurological perspective, it makes sense to pause between tasks—not to surf the Internet, but to do nothing at all. Meditation helps because it prevents us from churning away mentally during the gaps. It allows our brains to experience downtime as downtime.

A little bit of stress is good, because it presents us with stimulating challenges and keeps life interesting. Too much stress—prolonged, chronic, day-in-day-out stress—strains your mental functioning. It can affect everything from your memory to your ability to solve problems. If you have a lot of stress, you'll have more mental slip-ups: losing your car keys or forgetting where you parked your car, forgetting phone numbers and account numbers, coming to meetings unprepared or double-booking your time, and other gaffes. Of course these kinds of mistakes can occur at less stressful times, too, but probably not as frequently.

Prolonged stress can also lead to poor judgment, like failing to read the fine print on financial statements or taking unwise financial risks. Over time, these poor decisions add up to a lot of pain and heartbreak. When you function under high levels of stress almost all of the time, you increase the risk of burnout and place great demands on your physical, social, and emotional well-being.

Monotasking Hint

Take a moment to get centered before doing anything. This does not have to be a complicated exercise. Just take a few deep breaths and remind yourself to pay attention. When practiced regularly, this little discipline will lead to greater feelings of well-being. When you live ahead of yourself, always thinking about the next thing that needs to be done, you can't concentrate on the task at hand. That leads to an inability to do anything with the attention to detail that it deserves. At the same time, this forward-thinking takes the enjoyment out of the moment, because you are never really present. It's hard to smell the roses if you don't even notice that they are there. Breathing and centering also have physiological effects and change the body's chemistry.

You may have seen the signs of chronic stress in people you know. Maybe even in yourself. Such changes are notable: We often speak of someone being "not all there" or "not himself or herself." A formerly cheerful person becomes humorless. A coworker's quality of work declines. A friend reduces all activities to the bare minimum in order to sustain the tremendous amount of energy needed just to cope with the stress. Sound familiar?

Stress and the Human Body

To cope with stress, the brain releases hormones like cortisol and adrenaline, which increase blood pressure and respiration. You may feel like you're drowning or gasping for air. Anxiety and depression, closely linked emotions, occur as part of chronic stress. Feeling hopeless can lead to a downward spiral and an inability to recognize that stopping the stress can help stop the problem.

The stress response contributes to conditions ranging from high cholesterol to high blood pressure to migraine headaches to diabetes to stroke. To put it simply, living in a continually stressful state is like continually overheating your body. It breaks your body down instead of building it up.

A lifetime of chronic stress is suspected to be one of the causes of diseases of aging like Alzheimer's and dementia. Stress also suppresses immune responses, making it more likely that a chronically stressed person will be infected with colds and flu, and possibly more serious conditions. Common colds alone cost the U.S. economy $40 billion in medicine and lost days at work and school, according to a 2003 University of Michigan report. A 2010 Swedish study found that workers in that country averaged over five days lost per year due to the common cold and that reducing this number by just one day would save 528 million euros annually. The loss of sleep associated with chronic stress compounds the problem, as the body does not have sufficient time to recover from daily life and is more susceptible to infection.

Loss of sleep also compounds psychological problems. Not sleeping adequately is linked with impaired ability to learn and process language, and sleep deprived people have more difficulty in expressing themselves creatively and finding solutions to problems. The effects of sleep loss can be compared to the effects of overindulgence in alcohol, including trouble with executing tasks and slurred speech. Of course, everyone knows the feeling of irritability that goes along with not getting enough sleep, and this can become a problem if it happens too often. On a physical level, sleep deprivation may be one of the underlying causes of the obesity epidemic in the United States, since sleep helps to balance hormones responsible for the control of appetite.

That's the domino effect of chronic stress: physical and mental factors compound each other, sometimes with long-lasting effects. Stress is a coping mechanism for escaping from emergency situations. When the emergency recurs daily, the body begins to fight itself.

Yet we view this level of stress as normal—so much so that learning to live with a lower level of stress can be a difficult transition.

Becoming a Monotasker

Giving a single project your complete attention is a powerful skill when you consider exactly what our brains can do. You'll finish faster, produce at a higher quality, and find time—when it's over—to spend on yourself. Focus is the antithesis of multitasking-related stress, and with focus you will find peace.

Monotasking Hint

When making a to-do list, don't just jumble the items at random. Arrange your lists into areas of life responsibility: Church Building Committee, Algebra Class, Great American Novel. Take a few minutes to prioritize the items before doing anything else. Ask yourself, "In an ideal world, what would I do with this next hour?" Then make that item your first order of business.

Think about long-term well-being rather than just the emergency of the moment. Sometimes it helps to rewrite the list onto a clean sheet of paper. Completing the executive functions first (prioritizing and problem solving) will make doing the tasks seem simpler.

For all it's worth, monotasking can be boring, exhausting, and time-consuming when you're not trained to handle it. Would you ask your body to run a marathon after a career spent in a desk chair? Not without a little training. Then you shouldn't expect your brain to focus on a project for hours without wavering if you haven't given it the exercise it needs.

Meditation Is the Solution

The best way to train your brain for monotasking is through meditation. For every problem multitasking creates, meditation has a solution. What's even better, practicing meditation will help you be more productive, so you can find a better balance between work and everything else. With just a few minutes every day—and a commitment to making focus a part of your routine—you'll reverse the negative effects of stress on your body and mind, increase your creativity, improve your memory, and feel more relaxed and prepared for every day—all of which will make you more successful in everything you do.

Life coaches and self-help books often take a cold turkey, rationalized approach to time management and avoiding distraction. They tell you to just stop wasting time and pick yourself up by the bootstraps. They tell you to make a plan and stick to it—without giving you the internal resources to do so.

This book works from the inside out, teaching you to train your mind while you change the way that you approach the external world. You'll find that things tend to fall into place as your mental focus improves. As you change your mind, you will change your life.

"Believe that life is worth living and your belief will help create the fact."

—WILLIAM JAMES

Benefits of Meditation

When you first begin to meditate, you may wonder why you're sitting quietly and watching your breath. You will feel useless and restless, like you are, in fact, wasting time. At first, you will feel an overwhelming urge to go back to frantic activity, but this will pass. After sitting for a session or two, you will already begin to feel better, more content, and rested. Once you establish a regular pattern of meditation, you will feel happier and less anxious. The world itself will seem more vibrant, like you have switched from black and white to color. After still more practice, the nagging problems of your life will seem less severe and less important. You will work fluidly and intuitively rather than obsessing over the proper execution.

That's not all. Your mood will improve. Stress and anxiety will lessen. More tangibly, your heart rate will slow and your blood pressure will lower. Even your cholesterol levels will decrease. Research conducted at the Cedars-Sinai Medical Center in Los Angeles shows that meditation reduces insulin resistance in patients with heart disease. Over a lifetime, meditation will reduce your risk of heart disease, diabetes, and stroke. Meditation will also make you more likely to make other positive lifestyle changes, like eating well and exercising. The effects of meditation, which are measurable in themselves, are compounded as you start taking charge of your life and well-being.

In terms of the performance of your mind, your memory and concentration will improve. You will begin to see larger connections and patterns in your life that you never noticed before. You will see how small events fit into the grand scheme of things. This will remove some of the tedium and weariness of life. It's like hitting the refresh button on your own existence.

Committing to Meditation for Multitaskers

This book is designed for those who have active personal and professional lives and who have little wiggle room in their schedules. It is for those who can't drop everything and head for a Himalayan retreat, but who nonetheless want to reap the benefits of meditation in their lives.

Accordingly, none of the exercises in this book or in the accompanying CD take longer than twenty minutes. Some of them take as little as one minute. The program that this book teaches relies on many short breaks during the day rather than prolonged periods of mental exercise.

The program will also bring the insights gleaned from meditation into daily life: focusing on one thing at a time and bringing all of one's attention to bear on the present moment. Just as this program is about minimizing mental clutter, it is also about removing clutter from our lives in general, removing time-wasting distractions. This does not mean foreswearing modern conveniences or entertainments. It just means being more intentional about what you allow into your life.

A small dose of self-discipline will leave more time for the things that truly matter, bringing greater satisfaction. At the end of your study of this book and CD, you will find that you have more time for the things that you love, and that you are more focused and contented.

All you have to do is give meditation twenty minutes in the morning hours, twenty minutes in the evening hours, and a small portion of your coffee breaks.

When you are not meditating, work toward doing only one thing at a time. As you begin to practice monotasking and you see its benefits, you will not want to go back to the old distracted way of doing things. As the days and weeks go by, you will be able to sustain a single point of attention for longer and longer periods of time. You will feel your burdens lighten and your mood brighten, so be glad that you picked up this book, and get started today!

Solar Exercise

Record each phone call, text message, e-mail, and online post that you answer in the course of the day. You don't need to record the time or the conversation partner: Just make a check or a hash mark to note that the communication took place. At the end of day, add up how many conversations you had during the course of the day. Then reflect: Did your conversations bring you closer to the people in your life? Did they help you to get work done? Then give yourself a percent score for the day as to how many of your day's contacts were valuable. You may notice that you have some areas where you could be more judicious with your use of time. Don't judge yourself, though; just red-flag the problem areas and remember to be more aware next time.

Lunar Exercise

Buy yourself a pack of colored pencils and some drawing paper and make a sketch of your body from the inside out, the way you "see" it with your eyes closed. Notice that you still have an awareness of the location of the parts of your body in relation to each other even without having to use vision. You can still feel the boundaries of your skin and represent the outline of your body to yourself, and this is what you will capture in your drawing. This is not a body-image drawing, but rather pretend the "camera" is positioned inside your head. It can be pointed down, toward the chest region, or out toward the world, but it will not be positioned outside the body. Don't worry about artistic perfection, you don't have to show your drawing to anyone.

Then take a look at your drawing. You might notice that even when your eyes are closed, there are subtle lights or tracings of lights. Also, note how the chest is "down" in relation to the head and that you can visualize the entire world within the interior space. You may wish to repeat this exercise as your meditation progresses to see if anything changes.

CHAPTER SUMMARY

- Multitasking may seem efficient but it isn't.
- Multitasking leads to chronic stress, which can create a multitude of physical and mental problems.
- Meditation helps you to see problems in their larger context and think creatively to find solutions.
- Meditation provides the inner resources necessary to stop multitasking and start monotasking.
- Monotasking is itself a form of meditation, because it causes you to bring your full attention to bear on the present moment.
- Becoming a meditator does not require you to leave your responsibilities behind; it just requires short sessions set aside each day.

CHAPTER 2

HOW MEDITATION WORKS IN A MULTITASKER'S WORLD

If you're like most people, you exert a lot of effort in chewing on your problems. You probably think that your conscious, everyday mind has a monopoly on truth finding and problem solving. Most of us have the attitude that results only come from hard work, so we keep churning away at problems that may simply be unsolvable at that particular moment in time. Or they require a different kind of thinking or action. Your mind can be like a car stuck in the mud spinning its wheels. No matter how high you rev the engine, you still won't be able to drive it out of that mud without a different approach. You have to first get out of the car, then wedge something under the tires, and then you might gain some traction.

Discovery Through Meditation

Have you ever tried to untangle an electrical cord? If you just keep pulling tighter, the knots only get worse, and the tangles won't come undone. It's easy to do this when you're frustrated, but it's counterproductive. Sometimes if you pull in the opposite direction, loosening the knots, you can more easily see how to untangle the cord.

Inadvertent Meditation

As a freshman in college, when I had to write papers, I would sit at a terminal in the 24-hour computer lab and labor over every word, every sentence. It was then that I made a discovery that would make the work easier, for freshman year and for the rest of my life. When I got really stuck, I would put down everything and walk out to the university quad, a quiet, shaded area where I could stroll past the neoclassical facades of the oldest buildings on campus. As I walked, I did not allow myself to think about the paper at all. I concentrated on the crunch of twigs and leaves under my feet. I entered a quiet place in my mind. The quiet of the quadrangle lawn somehow entered into me.

Little did I know that I was actually practicing an ancient form of meditation. I later learned that the Buddhist and Christian traditions, and the Aristotelian school of philosophy, all had their own versions of walking meditation.

By the third lap around the quad, without fail, I had a "Eureka!" moment where the paper outlined itself in my head. All of this happened without direct effort on my part. All that was necessary was for my mind to untangle itself from its earlier exertions.

Active Mind versus Receptive Mind

It's like that with our minds, which have more than one direction in which they can go. Our thoughts have an active direction and a receptive direction. We spend most of our time in the active direction. The active mind solves a sudoku, thinks of the right word, makes a grocery list, and does anything that requires conscious thought. The receptive mind listens for a faint sound, takes in a painting, and feels the breeze.

Still other activities have active *and* receptive dimensions. An amateur golfer plays only with the active mind, while a pro golfer blends the active and the receptive. The same can be said for gardening, skiing, or most any other physical activity.

The person who thinks only with the active part of the mind will have difficulty responding to changing conditions and will be easily frustrated. The person who can listen and respond will be calmer and, paradoxically, more in control of the situation than the person who plans and attacks.

Meditation is about training the mind to emphasize the receptive dimension, relearning a capacity for listening, for wonder and awe. Meditation teaches us to set aside our own agendas and encounter the world. This can be difficult, because it feels like a loss of control, like giving up something, like taking a risk. It is indeed all of these things. But in return, we gain more vivid experiences and flashes of real inspiration.

Balancing Your Two Minds

Fortunately, you don't have to choose between the active and the receptive. The two go together like horse and rider, and every action on our part is simultaneously a conscious exertion and an unconscious adjustment to the surroundings.

The active and the receptive are both important parts of life. Meditation just brings them into greater alignment. This means having some periods where you purposely accentuate the receptive aspect, to make the balance come closer to 50/50. This will not come naturally, because we live in an age where action rules. It goes against the grain. If you have to sit on your hands to keep from reaching for the mouse or the remote control, that's perfectly normal.

"Contemplation enlarges not only the objects of our thoughts, but also the objects of our actions and our affections: it makes us citizens of the universe, not only of one walled city at war with all the rest. In this citizenship of the universe consists man's true freedom, and his liberation from the thraldom of narrow hopes and fears."

—BERTRAND RUSSELL

There's a difference between *receptivity* and *passivity*. To be receptive is not to be passive. Meditation is not tuning out or escaping to another world or even clearing your mind; it is setting aside anything that interferes with your complete engagement with reality. It would be more correct to call it *an escape from escapism*.

Seeing Clearly Through Meditation

In meditation, we set aside all fantasies about how the world might be, how we ourselves might be, and focus on what *is*. We see things with their blemishes and all, without judgment or comment. If we sometimes talk about stilling the mind or not thinking, we really mean that we see through the thoughts in much the same way as it is possible to see through the fibers of a blanket. Our thoughts color and obscure the world, and meditation seeks to unveil the world as it really is.

As you begin your meditation practice, you may find that some people get defensive when they hear about it. They will say things like, "Oh, I have a short attention span, I could never focus like that" or, "I could never sit still for that long." Of course, these same people could sit and watch a feature-length film with no problem or surf the Internet for hours on end. The real problem is not a short attention span, it's how your attention is directed and to what end.

If you're accustomed to activity and passivity, the idea of receptivity—the basis of meditation—can be uncomfortable. We notice the big, flashy things rather than the small, quiet things. Our senses are burned out by the barrage of images and sounds. The mental shell-shock of living in a consumer society means we have a hard time dealing with real space and time.

Monotasking Hint

Practice driving mindfully: Getting to work in a peaceful frame of mind will also get you there in one piece! This means not day-dreaming while you drive but focusing on the journey instead of the destination. Try to be as present as possible and think of that "wasted" time behind the wheel as sacred time. Don't weave in and out of traffic, don't cut anyone off, and don't run yellow (or red) lights. Above all, don't criticize the driving of others (as if it makes any difference!). Just be there in the moment, even if the road is uninteresting or ugly. If you are bored, notice the boredom. Even the most mundane moment can become a source for contemplation.

Meditation isn't just about fixing a problem or about coping with the frenetic pace of society. It is an alternative way of approaching the world—a different operating system, if you will. It allows for tremendous leaps of creativity, opening doors of possibility you previously thought impossible. As you begin to explore your own mind through quiet observations, you will see how many of your limitations are self-imposed, how many of the givens of life are actually self-created. You will see just how malleable your own self-concept can be. That will give you the freedom to explore the hidden aspects of yourself. You may suddenly find that you want to throw away your entire wardrobe or listen to salsa music or move to a new town.

You may also see things that you don't like about yourself. You may notice that you have a tendency to make jokes at others' expense, or that you can be overly glum and pessimistic. These habits are deeply engrained and will not go away overnight, but, as you notice them again and again, you can begin to change course. Just as a ship responds to the direction of its rudder, your outward habits will begin to change as you change your patterns of thinking. As you become aware of your negative character traits, you may feel guilt or self-hatred. Just let these feelings come and go, as you would any other thought that arises as you meditate.

You should now see the general outlines of what happens during meditation.

- Feeling a greater acceptance for the way things are and letting go of the need to control people and situations.
- Awakening deep intuition and creativity rather than focusing exclusively on rational thought.
- Exploring your previously censored self.
- Cultivating deep listening rather than operating on a preconceived agenda.
- Becoming one with your surroundings.

- Discovering and eliminating self-imposed limitations and opening yourself to boundless possibility.
- Diffusing negative character traits through self-observation and course correction.

This brief list gives a rough outline of the transformation that meditation can accomplish. You don't have to be an adept who practices for years on end. Anyone can realize this transformation. The results of meditation are not some far-off place that must be reached through strenuous practice. All of these goals are achievable in the here and now of daily exercise.

Monotasking Hint

Make a plan for your day and stick to it whenever possible. When interruptions occur, don't get upset, just move back to your schedule as soon as possible. Give of your time most generously to those aspects of your life that are more important to you. Then punctuate your day with meditation breaks and do-nothing breaks (stress on the *nothing*). Keep these breaks intentional and do not let them devolve into time-wasting. Reserve entertainment time for a designated hour or two in the evenings.

Selecting Threads from Different Traditions

The practice of meditation can seem confusing because of the overwhelming variety of techniques and traditions. Essentially, they can be boiled down to three different categories:

1. **Observation.** In this type of meditation, you watch your thoughts come and go, trying to slow their rate. Instead of identifying with your thoughts, you release them and see them as a byproduct of the mind's activity.
2. **Visualization.** In this type of meditation, you replace habitual thoughts (usually negative) with carefully selected positive ones. In theistic traditions, this might mean visualizing a deity or repeating a scripture passage. In other traditions, it might mean reflecting on an attribute that you wish to develop.
3. **Bodily Discipline.** In this type of meditation, you use physical effort as part of the meditative practice. Yoga and walking meditation are examples of physical disciplines. Most important for this book is breath control (*pranayama*). While nearly limitless variants of breath control exist, you can get the most immediate results by lengthening your inhalation and exhalation so that your breathing becomes deeper.

In this book and the accompanying CD, we will draw from each of these types of meditation to present a complete practice.

How to Begin This Program

Now that you have identified the problems with multitasking and have seen the benefits of moving away from it, it's time to move to the active implementation of this program. You will notice that your stress begins to fade the second you begin to make a conscious effort to re-order your life.

Breathing When You're Busy

The stress response causes shallow breathing and a rapid heart rate, which prepares your body to encounter a physical threat. Stress also triggers an emotional response that begins in panic or anxiety and can lead to sadness and depression. The good news is that controlling your breath interferes with this downward spiral and reverses it.

This isn't a la-la-New-Age promise. It's based in the physiology of the body. A complex network of nerves runs from the top of your head to the tips of your toes. This neural system sends signals at lightning pace throughout your body. You'll feel a change in one part of your body throughout your whole body. Losing a finger can lead to shock just as a wound in the abdomen can. Giving someone a foot massage doesn't just relax their feet, but sends pleasurable relaxation throughout their entire body.

In the same way, a network connects your brain, heart, and lungs. The interplay between these three organs prepares your body for any situation that it might encounter. Since it's a self-regulating system, most of the time you don't need to think about breathing. But you can, of course, take conscious control of your breathing whenever you like. This is where nature has given us a tool to take control of negative thoughts and emotions.

Monotasking Hint

Own a bicycle? Ride it. Have two feet? Use them. Slower means of transportation clear the mind and stimulate the body. Driving a car can be so effortless that it leaves the mind free to dwell on the past and future. The work required to walk or ride a bike diverts some of the mental energy normally used to cogitate. If you intentionally meditate while getting this valuable exercise, you compound the stress-relieving benefits. Take in your surroundings while you walk or ride and try to be as present to the experience as possible. If negative thoughts intrude, try focusing on a prayer or mantra.

Why Breath Control Works

A perceived threat will speed up the heart and lungs in order to prepare the body for an emergency situation. When you begin breathing deeply, you manually intervene in the stress response. The interplay between brain and lungs is not a one-way street. When you breathe deeply, you send an "all is well" signal to the brain that lets it know that it should slow the heart rate. You also send plenty of oxygen to the lungs. This sends a signal to the heart that it can afford to slow down. This explains how meditation can lower your heart rate and your blood pressure: more available oxygen means that the heart-lung-brain system can do less work to accomplish the same results.

You can achieve the same result by avoiding situations and thoughts that might induce panic. The stress response is triggered subconsciously; your brain can't tell the difference between a real threat and a fake one. That big report due Monday morning may lead to panic just as walking through a dark parking deck at night may. Multitasking also induces stress as the brain struggles to switch back and forth between competing tasks.

"Renunciation is always in the mind, not in going to forests or solitary places or giving up one's duties. The main thing is to see that the mind does not turn outward but inward."

—RAMANA MAHARSHI

Even if you can't avoid stressful situations, you can control how your brain responds to them. By breathing more deeply and slowly, you keep your system on an even keel and reduce the customary rush of stress hormones. You tell your body, "No thank you, I have this one under control."

Notice that this requires you to react differently. You may have learned to thrive on the adrenaline rush that comes from always burning the candle at both ends. You may be a stress-hormone junkie who needs that extra kick to avoid procrastination and get things done.

Once you start practicing breath control, you won't feel that breathless, panicked sensation. You won't feel the butterflies in your stomach or the pounding in your chest. Instead, you will feel something strange: a calm, steady feeling. The same things that used to provoke your ire no longer will. What might have ranked an 8 or 9 on a stress scale of 1 to 10 will now rank a 3 or 4. The result? You'll have a tremendous reserve of surplus energy that you can channel into finding creative solutions.

Breath Control, Step-by-Step

Deep, slow breathing begins to work almost immediately. In the beginning, try inhaling for eight seconds, holding for four seconds, exhaling for eight seconds, and holding for four seconds.

For deliberate practice, start with five minutes of breath work each morning and evening and gradually increase from there. In addition, anytime you feel anxious, do a few repetitions to calm yourself.

Build to inhaling for twelve seconds, holding for six seconds, and exhaling for twelve seconds. This will become the foundation for your meditation practice.

See how portable breath control can be? No one will notice if you are breathing deeply. You can do it in line at the supermarket, while driving, or sitting at your desk. To get the full effect, though, you will want to devote a few minutes each day to exclusively focusing on breathing. Feel your lungs expand and contract. Watch your breath flow in and out. Count mentally as you go. Once you have the rhythm down, you can stop counting and just concentrate on the breath. This practice has a cumulative effect—each session builds on the previous one as you reconfigure your nervous system. Your daily set point of agitation will change as you move more deeply into the practice.

Meditating in Small Bursts

You live in a world of meetings, deadlines, and projects, tasks and chores. You have a wall calendar, a desk calendar, and a day planner; a laptop, a desktop, and a handheld; a home phone, a work phone, and a cell phone. You have to pay the bills, clean the house, and mow the yard. You have to see to the needs of your significant other and your children. You have to care for older parents and plan for retirement yourself. On top of it all, you have to take care of your physical health by eating right and exercising.

Where is the time for meditation? There is so much to be *done*! That's why this book recommends short bursts of meditation to move you forward. If you're only meditating for one minute, five minutes, ten minutes, or twenty minutes, you will feel less like you ought to be doing something else.

As you begin meditating, your perfectionist self may want to take over and meditate for an hour or two. More is better, right? Well, no—at least not in the beginning.

Meditation is about increasing awareness, so you only derive benefit for as long as you are able to stay with the practice. The session should be long enough to stretch you, but no longer. If a particular length of time becomes too easy, move up, just like you would do with weights in the gym.

Even if you do decide to meditate for an hour at some point down the road, it might be better to schedule that hour in three bursts, including sitting, walking, and breathing exercises. Our brains, which work best when monotasking, respond well to carefully defined parameters and do not deal well with complete open-endedness.

Observing Consciousness

Most paths of meditation recommend watching your own thoughts as they arise, taking the standpoint of an observer in your own head, becoming aware of all of the words, images, and feelings that present themselves to your ego. That might sound a little difficult at first.

So what do you do to observe consciousness? A good preliminary exercise is to practice counting from one to five as you breathe. You can count on each inhalation. Don't worry about breath control for now: just breath normally. Concentrate on just the numbers one through five. As soon as your mind begins to wander, start over again at one. If you think about what you might have for lunch or the next item on your agenda, start over at one. You may find yourself rarely, if ever, making it to five. If you do make it to five, start over again at one. Avoid the temptation to count while simultaneously thinking of other things, as this defeats the purpose of the exercise.

Notice how your mind flits from topic to topic in perpetual activity? With practice, you'll be able to watch these thoughts as they arise and dwell in the spaces between thoughts. You will feel a sensation of opening, as if creating mental space. Indeed, the reason we don't have more peace in our lives is because we crowd it out, externally and internally.

This kind of introspection should be kept free and light. What you emphatically are not doing is psychoanalyzing yourself. You need not form any opinions about the images, opinions, memories, and plans that arise in your mind. However attractive the chain of thought might be, do not engage with it.

If you find yourself spinning out a chain of thought, gently bring yourself back to the calm center. If you discover something that you really must explore via conscious thought (and these occasions are fewer than you might think) put a bookmark there and return later. Don't waste precious meditation time with outside activity. Right now, your goal is to develop a receptive state of mind in which you attune yourself to your thoughts.

Keying Into Your Surroundings

A variant of this practice is to key into your surroundings. Listen to the subtle sounds around you. All silence is really composed of minute amounts of noise. If you are in an office, listen to the ventilation system or the hum of electric lights. It may sound silly, but these can become sacred sounds. If you are outside, listen to the sounds of birds and feel the sensation of the wind on your skin.

Meditate with your eyes open by taking in your surroundings without comment. This is a good practice for a lunch break or a coffee break. Just sit still and listen: all meditation can be summarized in this simple phrase.

Journaling in Meditative Practice

Many books on spirituality emphasize the practice of journaling as a means of understanding yourself and solving your problems. While there is nothing wrong with the practice—I've actively journaled for many years—sometimes journaling can cement habitual ways of thought rather than leading to new, creative paths. Journaling can become a kind of gripe session on paper. Instead of blowing off steam, it carves that mental pathway even deeper, making it harder to escape.

If you have journaled about a lot of emotional baggage in the past, consider a ritual to separate yourself from that negative energy. You may burn the old pages while chanting or singing a hymn; this can produce a huge sense of relief.

You don't have to avoid journaling, just be careful about how you approach it.

Silent Listening as Problem Solving

Once you have established your practice, you can use silent listening as a problem-solving technique. When you have worked your way up to twenty minutes of meditation per session, you can pose a question or problem that you want to solve.

To do this, simply say it: "How can I forgive my spouse for lying to me?" or "How can I resolve the conflict between my new boss and me?"

Then set it aside and do your standard twenty-minute practice. Afterward, you can journal to see if you have come to any conclusions. You may write the journal in the form of a dialogue with the divine or with your truest self. Just don't get bogged down in the journaling: again, keep it free and light. Rely on intuition and don't worry about finding the perfect turn of phrase.

Solar Exercise

Using a stopwatch or timer, count how many breaths you take in one minute. Then set the timer for one minute and try to take half as many breaths as you normally would. You don't need to hold your breath, just lengthen your inhalations and exhalations so that each breath takes twice as long. Take note of any differences in how the longer breaths feel. You may notice the muscles of your back and sides getting a stretch as they deal with the slightly higher volume of air. When you return to your normal breathing, your lungs may feel lighter and more capacious.

Lunar Exercise

Think of a time in your life when you gained some deep insight or epiphany about a major life event, like a relationship or a career change. What were you doing when you suddenly gained clarity? Get out a notebook and write a page or two about that experience. Try to include as much detail as possible: the weather, your mood, or the time of day. This may clue you in to your personal zones of insight, activities that help you to release the conscious mind and tap into your intuitive powers.

CHAPTER SUMMARY

- Meditation strengthens the receptive functions of the mind, enabling the meditator to flow along with events rather than attempting to control them.
- Receptivity and passivity are not the same thing: a passive attitude amounts to cultivating victimhood, while receptivity creatively responds to situations.
- Meditation is not "clearing the mind," but is, instead, refraining from escapism, seeing things as they are more deeply.
- Breath control intervenes in the body's physiology, causing relaxation to happen naturally.
- Taking meditation breaks makes you more productive by returning the mind to its optimal state.

CHAPTER 3

YOUR MEDITATION PROFILE

People meditate for many reasons: to enhance performance, to improve physical or mental health (or both), to develop creativity and intuition. Knowing why you meditate can help you reach your goals.

Identifying Your Meditation Goals

Are you a performance enhancer, a health seeker, or a creative thinker? Or are you some combination of these three types? Give yourself the freedom to make an unexpected choice. Perhaps you bought this book to bring more sanity and order into your work life, but now you realize that you're interested in the creative process. Or maybe you came to this book looking to develop superior mental powers but now realize that you would like to work on your sleeplessness. The chart on the following page will help you to clarify your goals. Just look in each column to see which goals most appeal to you. You may wish to highlight or underline the relevant ones, which will give you a personalized meditation blueprint.

MEDITATION GOALS BY TYPE		
Performance Enhancer	**Health Seeker**	**Creative Thinker**
Improve Memory	Lower Blood Pressure	Stop Censoring New Ideas
Improve Concentration	Reduce Cholesterol	Work with Greater Flow
Work with Less Distraction	Reduce Heart Rate	Increase Intuition
Decrease Self-Criticism	Get Better Sleep	Feel More Connected to Nature and Others
Reduce Workplace Stress	Reduce Anxiety	Sense Divine Guidance or Inspiration
Get Along Better with Others	Increase Energy	Visualize Projects
Develop Calm Under Stress	Improve Immune Response	Release from Past Habits and Memories

Performance Enhancers

Performance enhancement meditators are the most skeptical of the three types. They often take up the practice reluctantly. Their major challenge is to suspend disbelief long enough to see some benefits. Once they decide it's important, though, these meditators have little trouble sticking with the practice. The performance enhancer's ability to detect frauds, which abound in the spirituality and natural health fields, is a strength and also a weakness. A small dose of skepticism is certainly healthy, but if it goes too far, it can shut the door to beneficial practices. While performance enhancers can have trouble with dealing with the intangibles of the intuitive mind, they often make up for it with added self-discipline and perseverance.

Health Seekers

Those who meditate for health benefits may have little patience for self-discovery and spiritual growth. They, too, are results-oriented. They typically have more difficulty with life organization than performance enhancers, and they may struggle with developing a routine. They have the advantage of typically being more easy-going, because they prioritize health over success. A big struggle for health-seekers is seeing the results of meditation, which accumulate over time and may not be readily apparent. On the plus side, health seekers often already have a knowledge of physiology and the body-mind connection, which makes them more receptive to meditation.

Creative Thinkers

Creative types take to meditation like fish to water, but they may have a tendency to dabble in multiple styles and routines, which can diminish results. They may also trivialize the everyday aspects of practice out of a penchant for seeking the big, life-altering experiences. Creative thinkers will have no trouble with visualization and other, more tangible practices, but meditating on silence can be more difficult for them. If they can get over a sense of boredom with the everydayness of meditation, creative thinkers can surge into uncharted territory easily.

Knowing Why You Meditate

Knowing why you meditate can keep you focused on the strengths and weaknesses of your particular motivation. More likely than not, you fall into more than one category, but one will still predominate. All three types of meditators need to persevere, particularly in the beginning, when the practice feels awkward and is not yet incorporated into daily life. If you can maintain your daily practice for a month or so, chances are it will stick.

Poker players often have a *tell* that lets the other players know when they have a good or bad hand, and the others at the table can use this subtle information against them. Your meditation type is like your tell, the reason you came to meditation in the first place. Your ego will work against you by subtly suggesting that your meditation isn't producing the desired results. That part of yourself that wants to maintain the status quo does not want you to continue to meditate, because that might upset the way things have always been. If you already know that this will happen, you can prepare yourself for it.

- So performance enhancers will hear a voice that says, "You know, you have more productive things that you could be doing. . . ."
- Health seekers will have a voice that says, "You should probably just exercise and take vitamins. . . ."
- Creative types will hear a voice that says, "This is boring, let's go listen to some music. . . ."

These are just general tendencies, and the message will likely be even more subtle, tailored to your own life experiences. Your busy mind will come up with 1,001 reasons not to meditate each and every day. In order to defeat the active, conscious mind, you must be extremely vigilant. You must allow the excuses to arise and dissipate over and over again.

On an even more subtle level, the tendency will be to maintain the semblance of meditation while at the same time thinking about something else: the committee meeting later in the day, the evening session in the gym, an unfinished short story or painting. You can maintain two channels in your brain, one that repeats mantras or focuses on a chakra and another that continues to wander. On one level, this is completely natural and unavoidable. The challenge is to merge those two streams and go into deep absorption. With time, you will know exactly your own kind of mental wandering, and you will be able to say, "There I go again. . . ."

When your own tells become familiar, when you predict your own distraction and compensate for them ahead of time, you can enter into deeper states of meditation. You will be able to go beyond your type to the dark places in your own mind that you have never visited before. You will develop a self-knowledge that most people never have, and as this knowledge develops, the tendency to quit will become even greater. It is only when you face this fear of the unknown parts of yourself that you begin to achieve your goals.

To enhance health, performance, or creativity, you will eventually need to move beyond the surface level and get into touch with the deepest parts of your own being. Be bold, take heart, and you will get there.

Where and When to Meditate

As you begin your meditation practice, consider when and where you will meditate. Look around you for opportunities. For example, a neighborhood park may have a quiet bench for sitting meditation or some secluded paths for walking meditation. An office building may have a little-used courtyard or conference room ideal for a quick mindfulness break. That unused study or spare bedroom might become a little oasis, and a porch or veranda might become a hidden refuge.

Total isolation isn't necessary. Depending on your personality, you may be able to convert even the babble of a crowded train station into the appropriate white noise for meditation.

Look for Hidden Gems

Scan through the environments where you spend most of your time and look for these hidden gems. If nothing comes to mind, try driving to work a different way or going for walks around the house. You may find just the sort of place that you are looking for. While running near my place of work, I found a nature preserve that I had not noticed previously. It had a small sign and a gravel parking lot, and I never would have seen it from my car. Since then, I have taken many walks in those woods and have only passed a handful of other people.

Now let's examine your daily routine. How can you fit meditation into it? Can you rise thirty minutes earlier in the morning? Fifteen minutes? Ten minutes? Can you claim those first few minutes after arriving at the office, when you would normally browse through e-mails? If you work outside of an office setting, is there a time when you have few customers or clients? Once you start looking for downtimes, you will find them. As you begin to claim them, you will gain more confidence in taking charge of your own time, especially when you see that it enhances your productivity.

Monotasking Hint

Allow play and work to cross-pollinate one another. Take your hobbies a little more seriously and your work a little more lightly. The two will benefit each other in surprising ways. Could you make that report for work more lively by adding some color? Could you sing while walking down the hallway in the office? People might think you are a little wacky, but is that the worst thing ever? Conversely, could you work harder at household tasks, bring the spirit of the office into the home? Do you have 10 percent more energy to give to household tasks, as though your family members were important clients that you want to please?

A few caveats about building a meditation practice into your work life:

- Make sure your meditation breaks are breaks that you would be taking anyway. In other words, do your day's work, just be intentional about the breaks you take.
- Watch for time wasters more vigilantly than you ever have in the past. Guard your time and use it to the fullest.
- Be wary of multitasking, which robs you of productivity and peace of mind. Do only one thing at a time. Finish one task before moving to the next one.
- Use discretion in sharing your newfound interest. You're at a fragile stage where you may not be able to withstand ridicule or condescension. You don't need to be secretive, just choose your allies wisely.

"You are your own friend and your own enemy. You must work, but remain as if you have done no work."

—YOGASWAMI OF SRI LANKA

Meditating at Work

Once you have identified places and times for your meditation, you can begin to think about how to use these pockets of tranquility.

If you have an office with a door that shuts, no problem. Close the door for a few minutes and don't feel guilty about it. If you work in a cubicle, you may not be able to sit on the floor, chant out loud, or light a candle, but you may be able to play the CD that accompanies this book. If you can't turn off your computer monitor, go to an inspiring website (or at least find one that won't be very distracting). If you work on your feet, standing is no particular impediment to the practice of meditation. You will do the exact same exercises while standing, with the added benefit that it will be harder to fall asleep.

Maybe you are someone for whom the work environment is really not conducive to meditation at all. You can limit yourself to one- to five-minute exercises during the day (maybe during a natural break like a lunch hour) and look for longer periods at night.

Other thoughts:

- If you take a train or bus to work, use that time to meditate. If you have to drive a car to work, practice being mindful while at the wheel: It may save your sanity and even your life!
- Are you a student? Work meditation into your studies and see how your grades improve.
- Do you wait tables? Use ornery customers as a way to work on your patience and self-discipline.

Almost every life situation can be tailored in some way to a meditation practice.

Meditating at Home

Meditating at home often presents just as many challenges as meditating at work. You may feel like you're cheating your family if you take a few minutes to yourself. This is an excuse, because practicing meditation will make you more attentive to your family, as well as more patient and loving. You will seem more *there* when you meditate, because your mind will not be constantly going off in another direction.

The challenge is finding the right practice at the right time. During a seriously stressful period, you may not be able to do seated meditation. You may only be able to breathe deeply, while getting dinner on the table or paying bills at your laptop. Usually, though, you can find a few minutes at some point before bed. This might be right after clearing the dinner dishes or right after the evening's entertainment. You may have to limit some media exposure, but odds are you can find some time to work on your practice.

Gradually your family will come to understand why you are doing what you are doing, and they, too, will see the benefits. Don't expect anyone else to join you, though: If this happens, look on it as an incredible piece of good fortune.

Monotasking Hint

Avoid taking work home in the evenings and on weekends as a routine practice. If you must work at home, designate very specific start and stop times and stick to them. Reserve working at home for those big projects that only come around once or twice a year. When you're at home, focus on your home life.

Meditating in Other Places

I've already mentioned that you could meditate during your commute. You could also think about doing so while you're running errands. Take one or two minutes to collect yourself in the parking lot before buying groceries. Or duck into a quiet church or library on your way from dropping off the dry cleaning to picking up the dog from the groomer's. Use the places that already lie along your route. The loss of time will be more than made up in greater presence of mind.

Consider the rhythms of the year as you think about your meditation regimen. For many people, the holidays are the most stressful time of year, and yet because they're so busy, they're more likely to stop their regular meditation practice. But because the payoff at these times is also greater, plan ways to continue your practice. That can make these times as restful as they were intended to be. Other times of year may also be stressful, depending on your life situation: accountants may find tax season to be most difficult, and students may not be able to find time during midterm and final exam periods. Even if you can't meditate much during these peak times, perhaps you can take some time immediately before or after to prepare or recover.

Traumatic times can also disrupt your routine—and cause enormous stress. Break-ups, financial difficulties, loss of employment, bereavement, and other major life events make it easy to drop your practice, but if you can find a way to do it, you may discover meditation to be a solace. It won't fix these problems, and it won't even make you feel better, exactly. What meditation will do is to give you some time and space where you can be yourself and be with yourself. Meditation can help you to move through these challenges with courage and authenticity.

Pain and separation and aging and dying are, after all, normal parts of life that cannot simply be wished away. The moments of crisis, while they may be shattering, can nonetheless result in wellsprings of wisdom and maturity. You may not be able to change the circumstances, but you may find an attitude of dignified surrender. Yogis often call it *detachment* or *dispassion*, which may sound a little harsh when it comes to very intense personal situations. You may prefer to think of it as inner calm or solitude, a solemn acceptance of events beyond your control.

> *"Some people experience a mental breakdown that induces maturity. Others, suffering, resolve to enter a strong spiritual practice. Some become physically ill and then evolve into wounded healers, turning outward to help others after having healed themselves. And of course, many people in their experience of dying 'unconceal' their own natural wisdom."*
>
> —JOAN HALIFAX

Single-Pointed Awareness

No matter where you are in life, your purpose in meditation is to maintain *single-pointed awareness*—staying completely immersed in the present moment. All memories of the past and desires for the future vanish and the present takes on a new fullness as you remain with it in meditation.

You can accomplish this in two ways: engaging in only one thing at a time externally while entertaining only a single point of awareness internally. While meditating, this means only focusing on your breathing or your visualization. When you're not formally meditating, this means concentrating solely on the task at hand and giving it your full presence of mind and body.

When it comes to work, play, and any external task, this means moving away from multitasking entirely. When you're multitasking, two unspoken rules remain in effect:

- The first rule is that the most pleasant task wins. So if you're trying to work on a report at the office while also downloading music, you'll inevitably get more involved with the music downloads than the report. You may even sit and watch the status bar as it creeps towards 100 percent in order to keep from working on the report.
- The second rule of multitasking is that short-term gains will always be prioritized over long-term gains. The months'-long or years'-long project will always take a back seat to what needs to be done by this afternoon. Taking up a second language, for example, will always be on the back burner, on the fringes of your mind as those language CDs collect dust on your bookshelf. But you'll be returning all your e-mails—even the entirely unimportant ones!

Let's think about some of the implications of these two unspoken rules of multitasking. What gets done first is what *seems* the most pressing or what *seems* like it will be more fun. Most of the time, you aren't standing back to take stock of what matches your priorities; you just react to the demands of the moment without seeing how your options fit into the larger picture. Given these two unspoken rules, nothing new or innovative will ever get your full attention. If it seems like it might not return an immediate payoff, the multitasking mind will avoid it, always preferring to get a quick fix rather than devote its energies to something that may or may not pay off.

> *"The unexamined life is not worth living."*
>
> —SOCRATES

Finding the Time To . . .

Notice a subtle scapegoat effect here: so long as you continue to multitask, you don't have to take a look at those things that you would like to do but really "don't have the time" to do. "Don't have the time" is in quotes because you still have an awful lot of time to waste, you just waste the time in dribs and drabs rather than all at once. As long as you continue to believe that you suffer under huge burdens, you will never have the time to do what you really want to do.

The one thing that gets put on the back burner is different for everyone; for you maybe it's learning French or web design. Maybe it's calligraphy or tango lessons. Maybe it's physical exercise or perhaps it's this book that you have finally allowed yourself to read!

When you commit to monotasking, you say to yourself that if it is important enough to capture your attention, it's important enough to capture your *full* and *undivided* attention. You give yourself permission to explore those endeavors that have been lingering on the fringes for months or years.

When you give yourself the freedom to do the things that you *want* to do, you will find that you have more energy and enthusiasm for the things that you *have* to do. Monotasking, which might at first seem tedious and limiting, will come to be a joy as you begin to live in a way that is more in line with your true priorities. You will experience the rejuvenating power of feeling effective and yet also fulfilled.

Unwasting Your Wasted Time

When you monotask and meditate, you will notice that you have downtime when you don't have anything that you are *supposed* to be doing. You will realize for the first time just how much of your time was wasted with multitasking. You may not believe that now, but, after putting the material in this book into practice, you will begin to have empty spaces in your life. Avoid the temptation to convert these gains into more frenetic activity, or you will find yourself right back where you started. Use at least half of this time to do nothing at all—not even meditate. Create gray spaces that are not meditating, not daydreaming, not really anything. Allow yourself to go into a kind of mental hibernation. Your mind needs these downtimes in order to recuperate itself, and it is doing a lot of work behind the scenes when you least expect it. With any remaining time after meditating and doing nothing, work on those neglected priorities that you have been putting on the back burner.

Creating Gray Space

You may be wondering what it means to create *gray space*. It may help to think about childhood. When you were young, you could sit and watch the pattern of raindrops as they cascaded down a car window or observe the pattern of lichen on a stone. You could lie in bed on a Saturday morning and talk to yourself for hours or take a handful of sand and let it flow through your fingers. These kinds of in-between spaces are not exactly meditation and are not exactly intentional actions either. They are the kinds of activity that are most vulnerable to being edited out of our heavily scheduled lives.

You may think this is too hard on entertainment and the Internet, although this book hasn't directly addressed the topic so far. We take it for granted that the media and the Internet are here to stay and that they will be a part of life from now on. No doubt new technologies will also emerge. The question is how to gain the benefits of technology without suffering its drawbacks. The answer is to be cautious. Designate specific times during the day for the use of these technologies. Don't go beyond the scheduled times. Your friends and colleagues will gradually come to expect to hear from you during these times (and not others), and you will gain some sanity in the process.

Solar Exercise

Find a page of text and count every time the word *the* appears while timing yourself. Then find a similar page and count every instance of the words *a, an, and, the, to,* and *for* all at the same time while timing yourself. You should notice that it takes longer to search for more words. Try searching for *a, an, and, the, to,* and *for* on another page, but this time doing one word at a time. You should notice that it takes a lot less time to search for them sequentially than trying to do it all at once. You can also check for accuracy, which should be a lot better when you are only searching for one word at a time. This exercise demonstrates that monotasking is a lot easier and more efficient than multitasking.

Lunar Exercise

Review the information on meditative types earlier in this chapter. You know what your type is; now, try to imagine what it would be like to inhabit one of the other perspectives. If you're a health seeker, try to imagine what it would be like to be a creative thinker. If you are a creative thinker, try to imagine what it would be like to be a performance enhancer. See what you can learn by putting yourself in someone else's shoes. Thinking about the other types can help you to expand your horizons as a meditator.

CHAPTER SUMMARY

- Each person has a meditation type that determines why he or she decided to meditate in the first place but also comes with strengths and weaknesses.
- Performance enhancers are skilled at maintaining self-discipline, but their skepticism can be an obstacle.
- Health seekers have a knowledge of the mind-body connection, but they may expect results too soon.
- Creative thinkers are naturally drawn to the intuitive process of meditation, but they may become bored with the daily routine.

- Knowing your meditative type can help you to reduce your tendency to distraction by anticipating the ego's tricks ahead of time.
- Meditation can be a solace in difficult times, a way to cope with circumstances beyond your control.
- Meditation works by cultivating single-pointed awareness, which can be aided by making the most of down time and creating *gray spaces*, times set aside for doing nothing.

PART II

MULTITASKER'S MEDITATION PRIMER

CHAPTER 4

CLEARING A CLUTTERED LIFE

Meditation comes more naturally in well-tended spaces. You wouldn't study for a test at a rock concert, so don't meditate in a mess! Even if your mediation space is just a cubicle, you will find slipping into a peaceful frame of mind is easier and more effective when you're in a private sanctuary of focus.

Lessons for the Distracted and Disorganized

If you're serious about improving your focus, it's time to dig yourself out of the mess. You may have any number of reasons to justify your cluttered space, but whether you feel too busy to tidy up or overwhelmed by the extent of your task, you need order in your life! Here are a few tips you can use to beat the inertia holding you back.

Focus on *Micro*-Tasks

We've talked about monotasking—focusing on one thing at a time—but *micro*-tasking is a great way to reassure yourself that you're making progress. This tactic is especially useful if you're particularly overwhelmed by the work ahead of you. When you're ready to start, just break down the big job into little, self-contained pieces.

You'll progress through these micro-tasks one at a time until the job is done.

Unloading a dishwasher is an easy enough example. If you break it down into its component parts, your first micro-task might be to put away the forks. Micro-task two: move on to the spoons. Then you can put away the knives and the plates. This makes the whole task less onerous, because you can see the end of each little micro-task in sight. Those mini-victories keep you going until the dishwasher is unloaded. You may not do a little happy dance at having unloaded the dishwasher, but it is one more thing you've accomplished.

Micro-tasks are also great if you feel you're prone to distraction. By thinking ahead about the task at hand, you will be able to see exactly how you might get derailed later in the process. If you're cleaning your living room and know you're prone to end up on the couch looking at coffee table books, don't dust the table until the very end. If you know your kids are likely to need you several times in the hour you've allotted to tidying up, knowing what you've done and what you've got left to finish could keep you from giving up. As you start attacking those micro-tasks one by one, you'll start to see progress.

Micro-Task Everything!

Apply micro-tasking to everything in life, from cleaning your house to running a marathon to getting a graduate degree. Using this principle will lead to a life that is well-ordered and manageable. In whatever area you find yourself hesitating and struggling to be productive, unpack the difficult area into various different jobs with a number of steps.

Change Your Perspective

Have you ever seen a carnival strongman rip a phone book in half? As it turns out, you don't have to be strong to do it! The trick lies in the approach. If you try to tackle the phone book head-on, it will never tear in half. You might as well be trying to rip a tree trunk in two. But curl the phone book, and you will only be ripping a few pages at time if you start at the fanned edge. With practice, you can rip a phone book in half in a second.

This is another good example of micro-tasking, but it's also a reminder that you need to focus on what you *can* do, not what seems impossible in a task. Whether you're micro-tasking or just staring down a project from a new angle, a positive perspective will *always* help you push through to the end. There are plenty of ways to give a task a more optimistic spin; just take the time to figure out which one will help you improve your stamina. Here are a few that might help you muscle your way through the chore of organizing your space:

- **Think about the benefits.** A cleaner space is a more productive space! You'll be more comfortable if your home, office, or desk is organized.
- **Put on your favorite upbeat playlist.** Music conveys lots of emotion and easily sets a mood. Set your task to a lighthearted soundtrack to remind yourself that good things are on their way when you're done! For even more productivity, choose music with few words and keep the volume low. You will free mental space for the task at hand while reducing the sense of drudgery.

- **Reward yourself.** Rather than giving yourself an ultimatum that hinges on your failure, rely on the power of positive reinforcement. Take yourself out to lunch when you're done. Hit the snooze button a few extra times on Saturday morning. Give yourself a reason to smile when it's over!

Clearing a Path for Meditation

Organization serves as a useful complement to meditation. Both are practices you should keep regularly and both will improve your quality of life. As you begin to bring greater order into your environment through organization, your mind will settle down more easily, making it easier for you to meditate. Now that you know you can achieve a modicum of order and cleanliness, it's time to decide where your mindful sanctuary will be.

In an ideal world, we would all have a room set aside just for meditation, but you might not have that luxury. A calm, quiet nook at home or at your office will work just fine. Even one end of your desk will work if you prepare it thoughtfully. Make sure your space has room for a chair or cushion and a small table or shelf.

A candle or lamp is important, as the flame represents awareness; its steadiness will remind you of your inner self. You may also wish to burn incense, which serves as a reminder of the divine energies that are cultivated in meditation. If you are meditating in an office environment, you can use a subtle scented oil, something natural like orange oil, not so strong that it will bother everyone. You can also use tiger balm, clove oil, or ginger paste applied *lightly* to the temples and third eye. The sweet scent and slight warmth will help to lift you out of your egocentric self and into something larger, reminding you that you are creating heaven on earth through your practices.

Beyond these essentials, personalize your space with objects that are important to you and your mindful goals. If you have a divinity, chose a representation of that powerful being's presence in your way of life. The Hindu tradition has many beautiful gods and goddesses in its pantheon, and the Buddhist tradition has images of the Buddha and the Bodhisattvas. Christians may prefer a cross or an icon, while Muslims may desire a simple prayer rug. A jewish person may like to have some artwork of the Torah or a special *kippah* and *tallit*. Pagans may want to include the elements, such as a dish of salt or earth, or colored candles corresponding to the four directions, or a sprig of evergreen. You might also include a book related to your spiritual tradition.

If your religious life is not so easily represented, that is absolutely fine! If you come from a mixed background, feel free to mix and match imagery based on your personal beliefs. If you don't identify with a spiritual tradition at all, you can still choose objects that mean something to you. Whatever you place around you should bring you a sense of rootedness, peace, and well-being. Set out family photos or pictures of a beloved mentor or hero. Items that hold particular personal significance will be good additions, whether you look to your favorite jazz album, a child's toy, or a favorite flower.

A Home for Your Practice

As you're setting up your sanctuary, it is worth reflecting on the meaning of the home and especially the shrine you're creating. Your home is not just a neutral place: It is an expression of who you are and an outward model of your own heart. What you do with your home will mirror what's happening in your intellectual and emotional life as well. Philosopher Maurice Merleau-Ponty remarked that you know what sort of people live in a place within a few seconds of setting foot in their home.

Not only do you pick up on the individual details, but those details also combine to form an instantly recognizable mood. You may be so familiar with your home that you've stopped noticing its mood, but others certainly do, and it still affects your psyche all the time, whether or not you are conscious of it.

The effect a space has on the people inside it is so strong that businesses invest in creating spaces with good moods. Restaurants hire interior decorators to perfect lighting and ambiance because food served in an attractive locale tastes better. Office spaces are often optimized for the perfect balance of light, temperature, and personal space to improve productivity. These techniques work because all of our senses work together to create a vivid picture of reality in our subconscious mind.

The space in which you meditate will have the same effect on you and your practice, whether that space is in your home or elsewhere. So by creating a peaceful atmosphere, you externalize the qualities that you would like to see in your life. A home becomes a material prayer that brings positive vibrations into our mental states. For this reason, the home and its environs have a strong influence on the kinds of people we become.

No matter what you do or don't add to your sanctuary, make the space your own, and try to set it apart from ordinary activities. The more you let reminders of your multitasking creep in, the less focused you'll be when you sit down to meditate. Here are some dos and don'ts that can keep your space sacred, no matter how busy you are.

- **Do** keep your sanctuary scrupulously clean.
- **Don't** use a chair you normally sit in. If your sanctuary is at work, bring a cushion to put on top of your chair, but only use it when you're meditating!
- **Do** find ways to keep your sanctuary quiet and private.
- **Don't** use your table or altar for anything else! Remember that it is not a catch-all and that it should feel like a place *away* from the fast pace of your normal day.
- **Do** meditate at the same time(s) each day if at all possible— your body and mind will fall into the practice more easily.

An Office-Friendly Space

When you take your meditation breaks during the workday, you should have a good focal point for visualization and a reminder of what you value most. Before you set up a mindful sanctuary at your workplace, though, double-check your employer's policies on personal items. Make sure that your display is not so large as to make others feel uncomfortable or so small as to be easily missed. Find creative ways to make do in a pinch. So long as your space is your own, you can make almost any work space a haven for your meditation practice. Here are a few suggestions:

- Fill your space with traditional desk décor that you personally identify as calming and peaceful, such as a plant, a sand garden, or pictures of your loved ones.

- Put up a calendar full of images that matter to you, whether they're a collection of great pieces of art or photographs of your favorite destination.
- Give your computer a slideshow screensaver that scrolls through images that help you find peace.
- Set up a calming playlist on your computer or on a PDA.
- Carry a rosary or some other important item in your pocket to remind you of your commitment to meditation.

Your Sanctuary Should Grow with You

Remember that these suggestions for your space are just ideas: There are no rules you have to follow to create a meditation sanctuary. Use your creativity and make a space that matters to you. Everything you put in the shrine should have some resonance for you. Don't be bothered by how you think that space *ought* to look.

Feel free to change the space when you feel like it's getting stale, because change is necessary to sustain a practice over time. When you feel you mind wandering more than usual or meditation seems like drudgery, it's a good sign that you need to treat yourself to a special item.

As your practice develops, you'll also learn more about yourself and the things you want around you when you meditate. The physical culture of meditation—rosaries, lamps, statues, icons, and the like—are external signs that will help you maintain inward belief and focus. You can meditate without them, but it's a little harder to do. Allow your shrine to prime the pump of belief and motivation.

The positive energies of your space will eventually begin to transform the room and eventually your home or office space. The more you spend time in this space, the more you will begin to notice a calm feeling that this space engenders. It will become easier to meditate here than other places. As soon as you sit down in your sanctuary, worries will immediately begin to evaporate. Stop in for your designated periods of meditation, but also check in from time to time for one or two minutes. You may wish to bow, prostrate, or place your hands in *anjali mudra* (prayer position) when you pass the shrine, or just mentally say a brief prayer.

Clearing a Cluttered Mind and Heart

Clearing your external space is easier in many ways than clearing your internal space.

Wherever you go, whatever you do, your mind follows you, together with all of its frustrations and joys, tics and obsessions. Oddly enough, the first thing you need to do to get into the right frame of mind for meditation is to realize that you don't have control over your mind. If you have ever gotten song lyrics stuck in your head or had a word stuck on the tip of your tongue, you know how little control you have: your thoughts arrive unbidden and can create as many problems when you're trying to focus as they solve.

Meditation doesn't come easily to our willful, scattered brains. Just try to stop thinking; it won't work. Your mind will wander from subject to subject without necessarily any segue in between. If meditation were that simple, you wouldn't have to practice. The good news is that there are many things you can do to prepare your overworked brain for its mindful training.

"It's not that we fear the unknown. You cannot fear something that you do not know. Nobody is afraid of the unknown. What you really fear is the loss of the known."

—ANTHONY DE MELLO

Avoid Direct Orders

If you've ever tried to discipline a three-year-old, you know how easily direct orders can be derailed by diversions. I'll ask my son to pick up his books, and he'll just flash his most charming smile and point out a passing car instead. Just so, when you try to order your mind around, it will make plenty of suggestions to distract you. A multitasker's mind is particularly susceptible: you've trained your brain to believe that there are things that you could—or should—be doing other than meditating. You're likely to make a very long internal list of things to think about that would be more interesting than silent listening.

You need to outwit your own mind with the same tricks you'd use to motivate a three-year-old. Some of them are even the same tactics you may have tried when you got down to organizing your external space! You have to dangle carrots in front of it and promise that you'll reward yourself for good behavior. Remember all the positive influences meditation will have on your life. Tell yourself, "If I let this thought go, something even better awaits me."

Remind your mind to stay on task by gently bringing it back to center every few seconds. You must remain vigilant, or your meditation session will turn into a brainstorming session. Even if you come up with some good ideas, you will not find the contentment that is the goal of meditation practice if you don't practice disengaging with your thoughts.

Make Your Mind a Pathway for Thoughts—Not a Pitstop

The goal of meditation is not to stop having thoughts, but just to stop entertaining them. Become a corridor through which thoughts pass instead of a room in which they congregate. Take an observer's stance. Overhear your mind's internal conversations, but do not participate in them. With practice, a subtle shift will take place; you'll realize that you need not control your thoughts in order to master them. You do not need even to disown them, just stop trying to change their flow.

As you move even deeper into meditation, you will see that your thoughts have no author and that they do not originate with you. Rather, they move through you. Your thoughts have sources, but those sources don't include you; they are books you have read, movies you have seen, or things your parents taught you. These sources, in turn, have their sources, and on the roots of your thoughts can be traced back through time. You combine and manipulate thoughts, but you don't really own them. As you give up this ownership and accept your role as observer and translator, you gain a new freedom and spontaneity. You will lose the sense that you have a self to promote and protect, and you'll find that you can live in an unguarded way. With your internal walls down, you'll find it easier to focus everywhere—not just in your meditation practice.

Move Your Mind

Another strategy to gaining mental clarity is to think further down the axis of your body. You may have heard this technique expressed as *moving your mind, shifting your awareness*, or any number of phrases that instruct you to envision what's going on somewhere other than your brain. Focusing your mind internally helps you drown out external influences that could disrupt your focus.

Try the following exercise when you feel bombarded by the outside world:

Moving Awareness

Your heart is an important sacred site in many traditions and reminding yourself of its subtle, rhythmic influence in your life can help you clear your head. Move your awareness out of your head, down your spinal column to your heart region. Notice that you frequently think of your "self" as residing in your head, looking out through your eyes. To move the awareness down the body axis, close your eyes and imagine this "camera" moving down your spinal column, from the front of your head to the back, down the throat, and into your chest.

Now, visualize a white light radiating from your chest as you watch your lungs and heart expanding and contracting. With time and attention, you will be able to hear and feel the rush of blood in your arteries and veins; it will sound like a river moving through you. You will feel your pulse as well, especially in your neck. Bringing consciousness down the axis of the body moves you further away from the thought process that can be so insistent. You may even wish to visualize a wall or divider that separates your spinal column from your brain. Pretend that you are on the other side of a sound-proof barrier that keeps your thoughts in check. You may feel a bit silly doing this, but it helps.

Set the Stage

Commit to your meditation by setting aside the time that you have designated for the session. Turn off your phone, or at least the ringer. Put your computer on sleep mode or shut it down entirely. Jot down a few notes on your blotter or calendar if you need to remember something for after the session. Entrust your work to the universe, knowing that you will return to it refreshed with new motivation and insight. Turn off the overhead lights if you can. Play some soft music; use headphones if you're at work. If you are meditating in your home shrine, light a candle and some incense and say some prayers to your chosen divinity. You may also keep some fresh flowers on your altar to remind you of the brightness and vitality of the present moment.

Mindful Posture

If you will be sitting in a chair when you meditate, place your feet on the ground in front of you without crossing them, shoulder width apart. Sit up straight with shoulders back. Your back need not be rigid, but you shouldn't be slouching either. Your chin will be pointed just below level, your jaw relaxed, your tongue down or resting just behind your upper teeth, touching the hard palette. Put your hands in your lap, your dominant hand cradling your other hand, thumbs touching. This is called *cosmic mudra*, and it is acts as a kind of gauge for your attention. If your thumbs tend to press into each other, you are trying too hard; if they separate entirely, your attention has waned.

If you are sitting on the floor, sit cross-legged, or—if you have some experience with yoga or are naturally flexible—sit in lotus position or half lotus. You may wish to sit on a square cushion, a *zafu* (a round, Zen meditation cushion) or a thick book (a dictionary or phone book works well). Your back should be straight, or, more accurately, in a nice lumbar curve. If you ever have the chance, get someone knowledgeable to check your posture. For now, concentrate on being poised and alert. You may have some minor pains at first, but as long as the pains are not sharp or shooting, don't worry about them. Your back and core muscles will need to do some strengthening to make the posture more comfortable.

To keep track of time, use a stopwatch, egg timer, or guided CD. Cell phone clocks and applications also work, but they may be distracting due to e-mails and other attention-stealers. If you're going to rely on technology, disable all other reminders and pings so the only sound you'll hear is a soft tone reminding you that your session is complete. Try to avoid looking at the clock during the session, as hard as that might be.

Now you are ready to begin! You will find that silence is the best teacher. No matter how many books you read, there is no substitute for sitting and listening.

Mindful Monotasks

A few one-minute exercises will ease you into the practice of meditation. These can be done almost anywhere with little advance preparation. Don't think of them as throwaways, though. No matter how far you advance in your spiritual practice, you will always appreciate having a brief respite. You will also find that the same principles apply, whether the meditation lasts for one minute or one hour.

A Moment of Silence

Silence isn't just for funerals. Take one minute, sit in your meditation space, and simply listen for one minute. Listen with your inner and outer ears. Pay attention to the sounds outside and the feelings inside. Try to avoid making any commentary on the experience, shut off the internal newscaster. Absorb everything. Be actively receptive. This exercise, repeated often, will prepare you for longer periods of silence.

Just Say "Om"

Om is the primal sound, the sound of the universe that reverberates through all things. It can be divided into three sounds, A-U-M, which stand for creation, preservation, and destruction. If you are in a space that would allow it, chant the "om" out loud. Notice how you can feel it reverberating in your head, your chest, and your throat. Hear how it echoes throughout the room. If you are outside, hear the "om" in the sound or rushing water or the din of traffic. Allow the "om" to dissolve the barrier between you and the outside world.

I Am Bliss

Repeat the phrase "I am bliss" to yourself while breathing deeply. Remind yourself that you are one with the heart of the universe itself. Expand your point of view to include the entire cosmos. Think of the revolutions of the planets and the infinite reaches of space. You will emerge feeling more insignificant, perhaps, but also a part of something much greater than yourself.

All Shall Be Well

Repeat the prayer of Christian mystic Julian of Norwich, "All shall be well, and all shall be well, and all manner of things shall be well." As you say this phrase, dismiss all other thoughts as they arise. See how all things really will be well: problems are temporary, as is life itself. You will be reminded of how precious your life is and how fleeting trouble is.

Solar Exercise

Write down all of your areas of life responsibility and any relevant subcategories. You may have a category for "parent" that would include the subcategories "ensure good nutrition," "create safe environment." Or you may have a category for "project manager" that would include "assign jobs to subcontractors," "ensure completeness and quality," and "project a good public image."

Next, make note of those areas where you feel the most confident and those where you might feel you have more difficulty feeling self-assured. Take the most difficult area and make a list of five ways to improve. Also take one minute to look at the variety of responsibilities that you face each day and congratulate yourself for the things that you have done well.

Lunar Exercise

Make a floor plan of your home, including the arrangement of furniture in the rooms and the doors and windows. Note heavy traffic areas with arrows and low-use areas with shading. Write down three ways to maximize your use of space. Then think about potential locations for your home shrine. Perhaps some of the shaded areas could be converted into a space for meditation practice. Or maybe the congested areas could be relieved by redesigning a room. Discuss your sketch with family members and implement your plan.

CHAPTER SUMMARY

- Micro-tasking, breaking down each job into its smallest possible components, can help cut through the feeling of being stuck.
- Keeping your physical space free of clutter aids in concentration and makes it easier to meditate.
- Setting aside a personal meditation space allows you to enter a positive frame of mind more easily.
- When you're concentrating, simply allowing thoughts to pass through your mind works better than giving it direct orders.
- Good posture and breathing are essential to making meditation work.
- Moving awareness down the axis of the body and into the chest region helps you quell uncontrolled thoughts.

CHAPTER 5

SCHEDULED MEDITATION

Finding time requires more than just good intentions. It's one thing to have an intention to do something or say that you value a particular activity, and it's another thing altogether to assign it a space on the agenda for your life.

Scheduled Meditation

Scheduling meditation may seem a little unromantic, a little type-A, a little anal-retentive. But scheduling something means that it's important. Writing something down, especially writing by hand on a sheet of paper, has a powerful effect on the memory. By writing a schedule for your meditation, you commit to that appointment. You also say to yourself that you value your own well-being enough to take time during the day for yourself.

In the yogic tradition, the first two hours before dawn and the first two hours after sunset are considered the most auspicious times to meditate. This has to do with astrology, but it also makes sense from a practical standpoint. Before dawn, you haven't had the chance yet to get too immersed in the activities of the day, so you don't yet have to tear yourself away from your work.

After sunset, you have accomplished enough to call it quits and should similarly have little to bother and distract. Any later or earlier than these two time periods, and you are likely asleep or at least sleepy. So use these two windows if you can: not the whole two-hour bracket, but somewhere in those periods, find a few minutes.

What about other times during the day? How do you know when it's a good time to meditate? If you wait for a perfect time, it will never come. You will always have other things to do, and you may not always feel particularly inspired to meditate. In order for it to be effective, meditation has to be an appointment that you keep and not something you do when you feel like it. And yet at some points during the day you would derive more benefit from working than meditating, because you are clearing items from the mental landscape that would interrupt your peace of mind. And there is the usual business of life: meetings, reports, classes, and the like, which do not qualify as distractions and cannot always be negotiated. So you have to be flexible and work around busy times.

Finding Small Holes in Your Schedule

It's a cultural requirement that everyone should at least put on a show of maximum stress. But the average day is not a solid wall of activity—it's more like Swiss cheese. The key to finding a little bit of personal time is to look for the small pockets of air. Remember, we're talking about only a few minutes at a time. Most people don't have the luxury of big two-to-four hour blocks of time, but nearly everyone can find one-to-twenty minute blocks.

When you identify them in your own life, schedule them and commit them to writing. When you come to the appointed hour, drop everything and get settled for meditation. Beware that something will happen that might tempt you to deviate from the plan: you will get a phone call from a client, a deadline will be changed, your e-mail will ping repeatedly. Discriminate between the true emergencies that need your attention and the routine miasma of noise that should be avoided.

"The first principle is that you must not fool yourself and you are the easiest person to fool."

—RICHARD FEYNMAN

Maybe you have some trouble distinguishing between emergencies and noise. Ask yourself: "Can this wait for a few minutes? Will my reputation be affected if I don't attend to this right this minute?" Tell your obsessive-compulsive self that you can get right back to whatever issue arises as soon as the meditation is over. You may even have a better handle on the issue after meditation than you did before.

If you're still having trouble letting go, meditate anyway. It is better to meditate while distracted than not to meditate at all. If you miss a session because you just can't drop what you are doing, no worries: just get yourself back on track at the next appointed time.

Don't feel the need to atone for your sins by adding the time onto a future session: guilt tripping is not productive. This is about your own unfolding development and not about some imaginary yardstick of perfection. If you miss a session, it just means that that is where you were at that moment in your journey. So don't cry over lost time or a difficult season. If you have discovered meditation as part of the purpose for your life and not just an adjunct, you are not in danger of losing it entirely. You will come back to it at a later time when the life atmosphere is more conducive.

Making the Most of a Free Moment

The ancient Greeks distinguished between *chronos* and *kairos*—time as it is measured in days and time as it is measured in experience. *Chronos* flows in a linear, regular fashion, while *kairos* has connotations of the appropriate or fortuitous hour. When you manage *chronos* effectively, *kairos* will toss a few freebies your way. The big meeting will be canceled, the server will go down, or the boss will catch the flu. Without taking advantage of these gifts of time deceptively, you can use them for meditation and boost your productivity.

Notice that your old multitasking self would have never realized this gift of time because it would instantly be swallowed by the many-headed social media hydra of e-mail, YouTube, Twitter, and Facebook. Because you have consciously taken control of your time, you see this free hour as the gift that it is. Maybe this extra time could be used to push yourself a little further than you would ordinarily go in your practice, or maybe you could read an article or book chapter that would improve your technique. Perhaps you could go outside for a walk or look into a weekend getaway.

If you still have time, you could get to one of those buried priorities that you have been meaning to explore. Above all, give yourself a brief respite from the feeling of "I have to do this" and "I have to do that." Enjoy life for a little while. The hamster wheel will still be there when you return. Know that a happier self is a more productive self, so don't hesitate to give yourself a mini-holiday.

Advanced Meditation Suggestion

When you feel like you are ready, take a day off from work and spend it meditating. Find a state park, a monastery, an ashram, a hotel, or some other quiet place to get away from your routine. Tell only those who need to know that you will be gone, and do not attract undue attention. During the retreat, you might try sitting for half an hour, doing some spiritual reading, then taking a long walk. Repeat this cycle until dusk. Taking retreats will advance your practice by leaps and bounds, perhaps more so than any other single technique.

One reason people don't feel more rested is because they fill in the breaks with more information and more noise. Your brain may not process a blog post all that much differently from a report for work. It might be marginally better if you derive happiness from it, but you are still using visual processing, language centers, and other parts of the brain. If you are trying to write the report and work on the blog post at the same time, you are definitely adding stress to your life. In order for the brain to truly rest, you have to ratchet down the level of activity. Meditation provides a real rest for the brain because it brings it down to a baseline state while simultaneously calming respiration and circulation.

Putting a meditation break into your routine is like putting a period at the end of a sentence. It lets you wind down from what came before in order to prepare for what is coming next. Running on full throttle all the time creates confusion and stress.

Meditation as a Retreat

Occasionally nothing seems to go right: your holiday bonus has been canceled, bill collectors are calling, your boss criticizes your work, or your best friend is diagnosed with a scary disease. Suddenly you feel deflated and defeated. You want a stiff drink, a new job, or both. Where can you go when every part of life seems to be going haywire? Only one place: within.

At times like these, forgo the visualization or chanting. Just sit. Feel the pain and anguish without having to do anything about it. You don't have to fix things, you don't have to blame yourself, and you don't have to ask "why." Simply be present—or try to be present—to whatever is there in that moment.

Some of the self-help and New Age literature seems to be only for wishful thinkers. You know the kind of book that I'm talking about: believe and you can do anything, manifest prosperity (checks are in the mailbox just by thinking about them!), and other assorted fantasies. The flipside of this message is that when things go wrong, something must be wrong with you. So this message of prosperity and abundance is a form of self-blame (unless you happen to lead a charmed life).

Our thoughts do, indeed, become reality in surprising ways, but the world also pushes back against us, and it doesn't always care about our priorities. Sometimes things just happen. We can create the world inside our heads but we cannot create the world in general. The world can be a disappointing place, even for those who do their best to be compassionate and good. And at those times of crisis, the last thing that you want is someone telling you that it's all your fault. Often we are harder on ourselves than anyone else would be, and meditation can help you to forgive yourself and move forward. It can help you move beyond the often stilted analysis that you make of situations and accept them without comment.

An old Talking Heads concert video was called *Stop Making Sense*, and that's an apt description of what meditation does. When we make sense of things, we make them worse. When we stop making sense, we can have peace. *Peace* is not a matter of rainbows, unicorns, and cute puppies, or some sort of sentimental or naïve way of looking at the world. Rather, it's a matter of divesting ourselves of harmful thoughts and feelings, a subtracting process of peeling away the layers of mental accretions. We peel away the good and bad thoughts and emotions, because we have stopped trusting in our own capacity to discriminate between good and bad. Even destructive tendencies present themselves to the ego as good, so oftentimes the internal feedback can be misleading. Only with a lot of experience can we read between the lines of our own propaganda.

> *"Whoever cannot seek the unforeseen sees nothing,*
> *for the known way is an impasse."*
>
> —HERACLITUS

No Set Beliefs Needed

Meditation doesn't require faith in the innate goodness of human beings, or that the world is more good than bad or that there's a

God. For this reason, meditation as a practice appeals to all kinds of people at all stages of life.

If you've ever had a migraine headache, you know that the best thing to relieve it is a dark, quiet room. It doesn't take the pain away, but it is a good place to wait it out. Your inner self can be that dark room in painful times, a portable place of retreat that you always have with you. And when you think about that pain of a bad headache, you can't make it go away, but you can separate yourself from it. You can observe it as though it does not belong to yourself. And the same can be said of taking refuge in meditation. You won't be able to make those problems go away by sheer force of will, but you can stop identifying with your problems. In this way they become less solid and real, as though you were watching them in a movie.

Surrendering in Meditation

A kind of surrender takes place in meditation. You realize your own mortality and vulnerability, your own powerlessness. In difficult times, you can convert sorrow into sweet sorrow, the kind that reminds you that you are still alive. It may be scant consolation, but it may keep you from deeper distress or despair. All too often we magnify our bad situations by dwelling on them. Meditation gives us ease because it helps us let go of those situations.

When There Are No Answers

One of my friends in college committed suicide. She was bright and attractive, and would have made a great doctor or researcher someday, but she was troubled by a dysfunctional relationship with a boyfriend and probably some other things that none of us knew anything about. They held a memorial service on campus. At that moment, everything I had ever heard about suicide no longer made any sense. All of the psychological and religious explanations felt useless, even cruel. I came to the conclusion that some things just don't make any sense. A girl we loved was dead, and no one could change that or make it go away. There was some comfort, but even *comfort* is too strong of a word, in acknowledging our grief and powerlessness, but that was all. And time goes on, piling hurts and joys upon hurts and joys.

So if you can't do anything about it, why meditate? While there will always be suffering, meditation helps you eliminate *pointless* suffering, suffering that you can do something about. You can keep your own house in order, managing the daily ebb and flow of your thoughts and emotions, and you can calm, if not tame, your reactive mind, which always wants solutions to problems.

During the rough spots, sometimes the best thing you can do is take a step back and try to calm your frayed nerves. Meditation can be the quiet refuge that makes an untenable situation bearable. It can change the emotional filter through which you view the world to make the burden seem lighter. When you stub your toe first thing in the morning and then spill your coffee, everything seems irritating for the rest of the morning. The traffic lights seem to conspire against you, file folders rebel against your clumsy fingers, and the sound of a ringing phone makes you want to climb the walls.

This frustrated, persecuted feeling surely has no roots in reality itself but is formed by a mental process in which the world has become negatively shaded. By contrast, when you deliberately cultivate peace and compassion, traffic on the way to work seems to flow better, that annoying colleague just seems amusing, not psychotic, and the leftovers you have taken for lunch are the best thing you have ever eaten. This is not the wild optimism of intention manifestation or wish fulfillment or magical thinking; it is just the simple observation that our mental states change the way that we see the world. Taking control of your mental state can give you the strength that you need to keep going, which might be just enough to help find a solution.

Five-Minute Breathers

The following brief meditations can help you regain your equilibrium at any time throughout the day. Keep them in mind—and use them—whenever you feel the stress building.

Getting Some Air

Find a route around your home or office that will take you outdoors. Stand still for minute and take in your surroundings. Try to fully engage all of your senses: seeing, hearing, smelling, feeling, even tasting. Don't divide the sensations into pleasant or unpleasant, but just accept them without commentary. You can meditate while sitting on top of a mountain or in an alley filled with trash. Slow down your internal monologue and merge your attention into your surroundings.

Deep, Slow Breathing

Go to your designated meditation place and take a moment to get settled. Make sure your seat is properly arranged, any lights or music are properly adjusted, and begin. Set a timer for five minutes. Place your feet flat on the floor, close your eyes, and fix your inner attention on a point just behind your brow. Breathe in deeply for eight counts, hold for four counts, breathe out for eight counts, and hold for four counts. Keep counting your breaths until you feel established in the rhythm. Then you can stop counting, but try to maintain the same deep inhalations and lengthy exhalations.

Begin to focus on the outlines of your body as you experience it from the inside. Picture your body becoming porous and transparent as the boundary separating you from the outside world becomes thinner. Allow yourself to merge into your surroundings, and let your rational thought process dissolve. When the timer sounds, open your eyes. Take note of any differences in the way that you perceive the world after meditation.

Going with Gravity

Find a place where you can lie flat on the floor without being disturbed. Turn off the light (if you can). If you feel any discomfort, place a cushion beneath the small of your back, behind your knees, or beneath your neck.

Set a timer for five minutes. Practice deep, slow breathing. Become conscious of gravity pulling your body into the floor. Imagine gravity pulling any tension out of your body and pulling away disturbing thoughts as well. Become one with the floor beneath you, and imagine yourself to be an inanimate part of the floor. Pretend that you have forgotten how to speak, either to yourself or out loud. Allow yourself to rest in a state as close to mindlessness as you can achieve. When the timer sounds, try to take some of this interior silence with you.

Not This, Not That

Sit in your meditation space, either in a straight-backed chair or cross-legged on the floor. Close your eyes and begin breathing deeply: eight counts in, hold four counts, eight counts out, hold for four counts. Keep counting your breaths for four to six cycles. When you can maintain the same rhythm, let go of the counting.

Watch your thoughts. As they arise, dismiss them, saying "not this" or "not that" silently. Keep your negation simple without attaching any emotion or aggression to it. At the same time, keep your attitude expectant, as though you were waiting for something better than the thoughts your mind normally presents to you. Continue dismissing your thoughts, one by one, for the rest of the session. Don't worry if you have trouble doing this, just keep trying. When you open your eyes, note any shifts in your perceptions.

Solar Exercise

Make a spreadsheet that tracks how you spend your time. Include categories for different responsibilities at work, Internet activity/television, commuting, cooking, cleaning, running errands, and any others relevant to you. Keep track of time spent to the half hour for one month, and then merge your findings into a graph.

You will find that some categories consume a shocking amount of time, while others seem to disappear altogether (Exercise? Gardening? Time with family?). You can use this information like a budget, to set goals for the next month. Start slowly, only making changes by as much as 10 percent at a time. Select which categories you would like to expand and which ones you would like to contract and plan accordingly.

Lunar Exercise

Cook your favorite meal for your friends or family. Use nice linens and good china, if you have them. Light candles to set a relaxed ambiance. Sit down to eat together without television or other distractions. As you eat, be mindful with each bite. Notice the colors, textures, and flavors. As you talk around the table, listen to what each person says without formulating a response ahead of time. Try to stay engaged the whole time, and do not allow yourself to become preoccupied with other thoughts. Bring this same attention into our everyday meals, even if you're eating alone.

CHAPTER SUMMARY

- Scheduling times for meditation will lead to much more progress than meditating when you feel like it.
- In addition to the scheduled times, take advantage of unexpected free time and use it for meditation.
- Some seasons and times may be more difficult than others, but each phase of life has openings for living more intentionally.
- Meditation works by getting you to stop making sense of events through self-blame.
- The exercises in this chapter increase your typical meditation time to five minutes.

CHAPTER 6

SEEKING PEACE

Meditation can help you bring clarity to those moments when you have the least focus. It provides a powerful way to tame attention-grabbing technologies and make those distracting times more peaceful and productive.

Homing in on Your Multitasking Habits

To change a habit, you must first become aware of it. Coaches often use video footage to help their athletes see what's working and what isn't. For elite swimmers, for example, the slightest difference in the cup of a hand or the route that hand traces through the water can make the difference between winning and losing. When the swimmer sees the underwater footage, she can make the necessary changes to her stroke. A centimeter here or there wouldn't make a difference to an average swimmer, but to a professional, that small difference means everything.

By the same token, we can make ourselves more aware of our less-than-optimum times during our daily routine, the times we typically waste with distraction. Everyone has off days now and then; it's persistent slumps and slides that we are most concerned about here. How frequently do you:

- Find yourself staring at a full inbox, not knowing what to do next?
- Sit and look at websites, even ones that aren't that interesting, to avoid doing work?
- Go shopping online when you have no intention of buying anything?
- Obsess over social media (defined as checking it multiple times a day or multiple times an *hour*)?
- Go to the bathroom even when you don't have to go?
- Go to the candy machine or the snack bar just because you are bored?
- Sift through the same pile of papers three or four times without culling it or organizing it?
- Spend more time daydreaming about the future than living in the present?

Think about the recurring patterns of your own personal slumps, and, without self-blame, commit to analyzing them more thoroughly. You might start a simple journal in order to keep track of your time. Be sure to truly keep it simple, however, otherwise the journaling will take more time than the other time wasters. Try arranging a sheet of paper with one entry for each use of time: e-mailing, social media, websites, word processing, spreadsheets, cleaning, errands, cooking, etc. Then make one hash mark for each half hour.

At the end of the week, tabulate the results. Which areas surprise you? Are you spending way too much time on the phone? Is a specific kind of report for work eating up all of your time? The next week, you can try to do things differently in accordance with your values. Ask yourself: what would my ideal self spend a lot of time doing? Reading poetry? Writing? Meditating? Make sure that category expands each week, until it becomes a substantial part of your use of time. Make sure not to increase too quickly. If you do, you will find yourself in the same aimlessness that is part of the problem.

Don't be unrealistic either. Everyone will waste time: We are not robots. You will spend more time on the Internet than you probably should. The goal is not to waste zero time, even if we could quantify the problem to that degree. The goal is only to create more life satisfaction, more time to meditate, and to come to the end of a long day and be able to say that you did your best to live peacefully and productively. Nothing is more frustrating than having been busy all day long and having nothing to show for it. By actively looking into your use of time, you will be able to confidently get into better patterns of living and working, patterns that more accurately reflect how you think of yourself.

Monotasking Hint

When was the last time you ate in a restaurant that didn't have a drive-thru? When did you last eat lunch anywhere besides your desk or behind the wheel of a car? Challenge yourself to cook a nice meal this week and eat it at an actual dining table.

Why Persistent Multitasking Happens

Awareness of multitasking is the first step toward solving the problem, but it's not the only step. You have to understand why you multitask in order to stop.

Let's begin with the often recognized but rarely understood mid-afternoon crash. For many people, this is a very unfocused and unproductive time. The popular myth has it that digesting your lunch causes the mid-afternoon lag and you can solve it with power naps and energy drinks. Not that there's anything inherently wrong with power naps and energy drinks, but they don't solve the underlying problem of finding intrinsic motivation in what you do. In order to get beyond the slump, you'll need to look at the habits that might be contributing to the problem.

Here are some observations to keep in mind when trying to beat the slump:

1. **You seek entertainment at work not because you're lazy, but because you're bored.** The first way to beat boredom is to recognize it as a friend and stop trying to avoid it. Boredom, which is a subtle form of avoidance, should tell you that a particular task does not give you immediate gratification, but it should also tell you that the task is not all that difficult. If you can get bored doing something, chances are you can knock it out in a brief but focused effort. Instead of trying to escape the difficulty, go into monotasking mode until it is done. This is more than just "getting it out of the way": enter into that task with every fiber of your being and don't just rush through it so that you can move on to something else. When you immerse yourself with complete and

total attention in the previously undesirable work, you will become interested in it and take pride in it. The time will begin to fly by, no matter how mundane the chore. Undertake the work from a sense of service to others. Harness the good feelings that you have gained from meditation and put them into the work.

2. **When you multitask, you're not setting clear priorities, which leads to lower productivity and a lowered emotional state.** A kind of domino effect happens as the day wears on. When you try to tackle several projects at once, each one moves at a snail's pace. Work that did not have to be drudgery now becomes drudgery, because you have little sense of accomplishment. To escape from this sense of futility, you pursue distractions (usually in the form of infotainment), further compounding the problem. The afternoon goes by, very little gets done, and feelings of stress and being behind the eight ball accumulate. Then the whole cycle carries over into the next day.

3. **Meditation is a better alternative than infotainment.** For one thing, meditation doesn't have the addictive quality that electronic distractions do. It's the opposite of mindlessly clicking on links. The mindfulness that results from taking a few minutes to meditate will lead to greater ability to concentrate. Meditation is the break that allows you to return to work better prepared to meet challenges, while web surfing is the break that allows you to take more breaks while never fully recuperating.

4. **When you don't decide what is the most important use of your time, slumps result.** When executive decision-making

(prioritizing and problem-solving) hasn't happened yet, the resulting fog prevents further progress. Jobs must be broken down into small parts before they can be managed effectively. In the same way that you would, when observing your thoughts, observe the task to be completed and allow it to resolve into micro-tasks. Take the emotional charge out of the job and see it as though someone else were doing it. Regard yourself and the task to be done in the third person, from the standpoint of an observer. When you can see the task for what it is, it will fit more easily into your life and values system.

5. **Distractibility masks a subtle defeatist attitude.** Distraction and depression are often closely correlated, because the depressed person secretly believes that nothing is worth accomplishing anyway. Often depression is coupled with a kind of fatalism in which someone believes that they really can't do much to improve their lives. In that case, it doesn't matter if you watch YouTube all day instead of getting your work done.

Taking Charge of Your Time

Distraction relies on the weak points, the unscheduled, vague parts of our lives to wreak its havoc. Having a few simple targets to meet can keep distraction at bay most of the time. Make a game of doing a few distasteful things each day, those annoying tasks that get your emotional self going. Over time, you will begin to enjoy the feeling of not getting bogged down in the painful details.

Taking charge of your time is apt to require some goal-setting and some checklists: we have to concede that much to the time management gurus. Failing to meet a particular goal is not, however, a problem in itself. Only protracted, ongoing failure to meet a particular set of goals is apt to cause problems in life and derail the attempt to find peace and well-being. The key is, rather, to understand the conditions that give rise to the failure to meet a particular goal. Once you understand the underlying causes, you will be able to better address the problem. No amount of self-flagellation can achieve that, it only comes through greater awareness and self-reflection. The solution that finally comes will be more natural, in balance with changing circumstances and your own personal disposition. You can't push a leaf upstream forever, and you can't go against the grain of your own personality forever. We all have to find our own styles of living and working, our own ways of getting around obstacles and being productive.

You may not be multitasking for all of the reasons on this list, but if you're honest, you will probably see yourself reflected in at least some of them. Know that you are in good company, because even those with the most invulnerable exteriors—corporate CEOs and elite athletes—struggle to maintain motivation and a sense of balance in life. As soon as you begin to face your lack of motivation, you have already made it halfway to the goal. Knowing your own tendencies allows you to overcome them, no matter how dire the situation. You will find yourself with a new enthusiasm as soon as you set your mind to tackle the problem.

"If I have ever made any valuable discoveries, it has been due more to patient attention than to any other talent."

—ISAAC NEWTON

Getting The Peskiest Tasks Done

When a particular task always gets shuffled to the bottom of your list, when it makes you groan just thinking about it, when it seems so awful as to be the antithesis of everything right and good (like filing your tax return, perhaps? Folding laundry? Creating a new spreadsheet?), you still have options.

The Ten-Minute Rule

As long as you are not at or beyond the deadline for a particular project, employ the ten-minute rule. Set a timer for ten minutes and make yourself work on the unpleasant task for ten minutes. It's hard to commit to an hour or two, but it's easier to commit to ten minutes. Ten minutes is enough to get you started and maybe, just maybe, you'll keep working when the ten minutes is up. Keep doing this every day and you will make real progress.

The Exclusion Rule (AKA The Nuclear Option)

If it's already too late for the ten-minute rule, bring out the nuclear option—the exclusion rule. The exclusion rule means that you will do nothing except the unpleasant thing until it is finished. No computer games, no e-mail, no phone calls, no to-do lists, no other projects, no Facebook, no filing, nothing until you have done what you don't want to, but really need to, do. Once you start doing the thing that you don't want to do, whether it's paying bills or going to the gym or writing a book review or learning HTML, it won't be all that bad. You will see that what you have built up into a huge pain wasn't worth all the consternation.

Monotasking Hint

Consider starting a television-free night at your house. Designate one night a week to turn off the television. Play a game together as a family, do a puzzle, or read books. You will be surprised that you are more entertained and enjoy each other's company.

What Next?

If neither of these strategies works, ask yourself, "What are you protecting?" Somewhere in the refusal to get things done is an ego that wants to be indulged, a self that wants to be protected from the banality and mess of the world.

A regular meditation practice will help you see that that childish self is not the real you. The real you is beyond words and cannot be harmed, bored, humiliated, or otherwise degraded. Meditation will help you see that what seems like a hardship is really a triviality, and that you're giving it more weight and emotional attention than it deserves. If you bring mindfulness and one-pointed awareness to your day, you will accomplish more than ever before while simultaneously bringing more peace into your life. You will not be coping with chronic worries about what you're not getting done and what you're resisting doing.

Focus Where You Need It Most

While the mid-afternoon slump represents a typical time for above-average distraction, lack of productivity, and low emotional states, you'll want to take a look at your own experience and identify those times when you multitask and when you feel low and unmotivated.

What Is Motivation?

It's worth thinking about motivation itself, which we tend to make into a mysterious force that we either have or don't have. It's better to think of a lack of motivation as a pattern of thinking, made manifest in mental phrases like, "I just don't have any energy," "It wouldn't do any good anyway," "I don't know what I should do next," "I guess I'm just lazy," and "I don't feel like it." These thought patterns become self-fulfilling prophecies that result in blankly staring at the computer screen, taking multiple trips to the coffee station or the snack machine, and rampant entertainment "fixes."

Finding Motivation, Part 1

One way to find motivation, *grade B motivation*, is to think about how you would feel better once "X" was accomplished, or how you would feel better if you just focused on one thing at a time and did a task until it was done. Imagine yourself completing the report, making the phone calls, or whatever has you bogged down. This kind of motivation is based on *extrinsic* reward, the feeling of payoff.

Another kind of extrinsic reward is to say, "If I get this done, I can go out to lunch today," or "If I can read the next fifty pages, I'll get a candy bar." There is nothing wrong with treating yourself, but extrinsic motivation has some serious drawbacks. First, you may not always have a sense of accomplishment or payoff every time something gets done, especially when it comes to those mundane tasks that must be done every day or every week. Second, you can't always afford to lose the time or even the money to treat yourself. So it's better to rely on *grade A* or *intrinsic* motivation.

Advanced Meditation Suggestion

Try sitting in lotus posture. Grab one foot and pull it up so that it rests on the opposite thigh, as close to the hip joint as you can get it. Then pull up the other foot and rest it on the opposite thigh, or on the calf if you can't get it to go that far. The result should be a stable, tightly locked posture. You may only be able to hold the pose for a few seconds at first. Try to work your way toward one minute, five minutes, twenty minutes, and then thirty minutes. Some stretching pain is normal, but stop if you have a sharp pain in your muscles or joints. If you can master the lotus position, your feet will be less likely to fall asleep, and you will achieve better posture while meditating.

Finding Motivation, Part 2

Intrinsic motivation is different from just feeling like doing something. Rather, intrinsic motivation views feelings as just another form of extrinsic motivation, like giving a kid a lollipop for setting the table. Feelings can be misleading, because a good or bad feeling can accompany almost anything. Just because you don't feel all bubbly and gushy inside doesn't mean that you aren't doing the right thing. Conversely, a warm fuzzy feeling may accompany something that really isn't the best use of resources.

That doesn't mean that we should become zombies, ignoring our feelings altogether; it just means that feelings don't get to determine the agenda. Intrinsic motivation places a priority on positive action and seeks to ingrain such action in habit, so that it becomes automatic. Intrinsic motivation allows you to do something day after day, week after week, year after year, regardless of whether or not you feel like doing it. You show up at the writing desk, at the time clock, at the gym, at the kitchen sink, no matter what.

When action becomes ingrained in habit, self-created drama disappears and obstacles are cleared before they ever arise. You're already doing the work before the whining, self-pitying voice ever gets started.

Meditation Is Action

What does all of this have to do with meditation? Well, meditation is a form of action, not an escape or a distraction. Meditation hones the razor-sharp focus that you need to do things well, and the attitude and insight you need to ignore emotions and false beliefs. Meditation allows you to see when you have encountered a genuine problem and when you're dealing with a drama created by the ego. It helps you cut through the addiction to extrinsic reward and find satisfaction in the present moment. It also helps you stop worrying. If you lack a feeling of satisfaction when you do your work, it doesn't mean anything huge or important. If you feel that no one notices the work that you have done, you don't dwell on the feeling.

Meditation will not magically carry the day for you, but it will help you to work at your best, channeling all of your energies into a single objective.

Could you achieve the same results by monotasking alone, without meditation? Yes, but your results wouldn't be as good. Seeding the day with meditation breaks leads to fewer distractions, because meditation sharpens the mind and gives it the ability to decompress and fine-tune itself. Your work will go faster because it is not hampered by competing concerns.

Breaking Your Multitasking Habit

After years of ingrained habit, it can be hard to go from multitasking to monotasking, from frantic activity to periodic meditation. This transition requires persistence and a forgiving attitude. You may catch yourself trying to send an e-mail while talking on the phone, or running a social media application in the background of your desktop. Each time this happens, just get centered again in one activity. No need for self-blame or commentary; just move back to the thread of singular activity again. The same exact principle holds for meditation: each time you find yourself wandering down one of the rabbit paths of the mind, get back to the calm center.

Getting grounded doesn't mean you'll never get distracted. You just become better at catching yourself in the act and coming back to center. A serious multitasker wastes hours a day by switching back and forth between tasks. You can cut that down to minutes. Your eventual goal is to never waste a single minute.

But what counts as waste? If you love organizing your sock drawer, and it's important to you that it be organized, you have not wasted time doing that. If you love collecting stamps, it's not wasting time to work on your stamp collection. But you must find clarity between love and addiction. If you "love" World of Warcraft so much that you stop taking showers and going to the bathroom, something pathological is happening.

Meditation gets us to take a hard look at ourselves, to say inwardly, "Is this *really* making me happy?" Or maybe to ask, "Is this habit making my life better? Does it make me a better person?" Don't let this introspection go on too long (for introspection, too, can be a bad habit). Just do a brief check and move on.

Suppose you don't put that distraction down right away: that's just something else to notice. Don't judge: just watch yourself wasting time. Eventually, you will see the undesirability of going down that path and you'll do something else.

Maybe you're thinking, "But I can't give up X...." You don't have to give anything up. If it is frivolous and shallow, fine! Just realize that you're choosing to spend your time on that activity and do it intentionally. Don't let the hours slip between your fingers unnoticed. Do something with them! If you need to have a designated time to surf random websites, then create one. The goal here is becoming more conscious of your use of time and attention.

Think about what in your life you want to grow and expand and what you want to atrophy and die. Give breathing room to those things that you want to encourage—lavish your time and attention on these priority items. If you feel a little reckless doing this, that's okay. How else can you create a strong habit unless you deviate from your old, restrictive form of life?

Say you want to do something a bit off the beaten path, like salsa dancing or skydiving. Give that interest hours of your time and a chunk of your budget. Explore it. When you realize that your free time will be spent on this thing that you love, you won't mind letting go of a few time-wasters and diversions. Why? Because they aren't as interesting.

Letting go of multitasking isn't some kind of grim discipline. In fact, most people find it to be a relief that they can get everything done that needs to be done without doing three or four things at a time. In fact, it's much easier to monotask once you get over the initial feeling of listlessness. You may have a little bit of nervousness at first, like you are missing something important, but that will give way to enjoyment when you have time for your true priorities.

In order to have peace in life, the way you spend your time must match your priorities. You must also give yourself the downtime to recuperate from your efforts. Those stretches of time shrink with every unnecessary diversion, and some marketer or blogger is always more than willing to fill the empty spaces. If you want to have peace, you have to love the empty spaces and live into them, not with frantic busyness, but with thoughtful engagement.

More Five-Minute Monotasks

Let's look at some other simple ways you can train yourself to do the monotasking that will bring peace to your life.

Forming an Intention

Otherwise known as *creative visualization*, forming an intention for the day (or part of the day) can help guide your mind down the right path. Set a timer for five minutes, do some deep breathing, and allow your mind to reflect on the particular course of action that you would like to achieve. Picture plans falling into place, coworkers helping you to achieve your goals, and the complete cooperation of people and circumstances. Put all your mental energy into believing in this ideal vision. Note any resistance or skepticism.

When the timer sounds, say a brief prayer for the realization of this vision. When you open your eyes, make a plan on paper for your intention, and stick to the plan as much as possible. You will be surprised by the results.

Meditating on Animals and Nature

Find a place to sit outdoors and simply observe. Watch the way a tree limb curves to direct light to the leaves. Listen to birds address each other. Watch squirrels as they scamper in play. Notice that you, too, belong to this world, that you're not separate from it. You may sense tension releasing, an insight forming. Don't force it. Be receptive, open, listening, and let the experience happen. You don't have to control and manipulate everything. As you become more animal, more natural, things have a way of coming together. Return to your day more refreshed and aware, less hampered by worries.

Combating Negativity

Maintaining mental discipline can be difficult for anyone. Occasionally, sadness or other negative thinking or feeling will arise. I'm not talking about appropriate sadness here—the kind that comes when a pet dies. I'm talking about sadness or negativity that's accompanied by a sense of futility and worthlessness.

In this five-minute meditation, take a look at the feeling and observe it. Notice how it feels physically. You may have a knot in your stomach, a lump in your throat, that sinking feeling in your chest. Notice how it feels emotionally. You may have a specific, repetitive script in your mind: "I'm worthless, I can't do anything right."

Stand apart from the sadness and see it mentally. Give it a shape and a color—like a dark spot covering your heart. Notice that this feeling is not you; it may live inside your body, but it is an unwelcome guest. You may stop simply with observing or, if you feel up to it and have the time, see a bright white light radiating from deep within—a light of peace, joy, and love. See the mighty white light of your truest Self overcoming that momentary darkness. When you emerge from meditation, the sadness may still be there, but it will not seem so overwhelming. Repeat the exercise as often as necessary.

Coffee Break

Put a note on your favorite coffee cup that says "No time wasted" or "Pay attention." Each time you get a cup of coffee, spend five minutes meditating. You will be surprised at how the breaks add up. Keep a note pad beside your coffee cup to briefly record any insights gained.

Ten-Minute Monotasks

Some exercises take a little longer to do but are worth carving a little extra time out of your day for.

Go For a Walk

Leave your work behind for ten minutes and find a good place to walk. Do not bring a music player, cell phone, or any other device. Lock them in a drawer or in the glove compartment of your car, if need be. Make an effort to disengage from the concerns of the day. Paying attention to your surroundings will help. Whether you are walking on a residential street, through an office park, or on a busy thoroughfare, key into the sights, sounds, and smells around you. Pretend for a second that there is nowhere else in the world that you would rather be, that this place, wherever it might be, is secretly heaven on earth.

Allow your surroundings to affect you. Turn up the volume on your sensations and turn down the volume on other thoughts. Try to feel intensely, as though each leaf on every tree, each reflection on every car bumper, had a message to convey to you. Listen deeply, as though everything in the world depended on these ten minutes and what they have in store for you. Make the most of the time: be alert and fully present. When you return from your walk, see if you have a different take on things. Jot down any shift in perspective, any ideas that might have shaken loose during that time. See if you can bring that same heightened awareness into the rest of the day.

Sacred Word

As you develop your powers of concentration, you will be able to stay in the present moment for longer periods of time. Find a sacred word, like *peace, joy, calm,* or even *now* and use it to bring yourself back when your thoughts wander. After selecting your sacred word, set a timer for ten minutes. Repeat the sacred word and concentrate on your breath. Allow the feeling of the word to dispel noise and sharpen your focus. If you find yourself getting antsy, trace the sources of your restlessness. Observe your internal dialogue and don't feel the need to act on it. If you can resist distraction for a few seconds, it will go away. At the end of the ten minutes, see if the sacred word has become more of a reality in your life. Keep working with the word throughout the day and see if you can quiet your interior monologue.

Pen and Paper

Find a good pen and some paper. Write a letter to a friend, a journal entry about the day's events, or a description of a new initiative. Follow the flow of thoughts as they make their way onto the page. Stop and doodle if you like, or write in fragments and bullet points. Keep writing until you have filled a page or two. Do this whenever your mind feels full or hazy and see the clarity that it brings.

One-Minute Refreshers

When you don't have even five or ten minutes, try the following mindfulness exercises. They each only take one minute.

- **Flora Session.** Put a single flower or a sprig of greenery in your workspace. Reflect on the silent life of plants, the way they grow without care. Look at your little sample of botanical life and absorb its silent beauty. Take on its qualities as you go about the day.

- **Harnessing Memory.** Think of a person who embodies wisdom and grace for you. Remember that person in very concrete terms: the wrinkles around your grandmother's eyes, the cherubic smile of a spiritual preceptor, the knowing quip of a college mentor. Allow some of the qualities of that person to rub off on you as you take a brief break.

- **Reaching Out.** Mentally send your love and concern to someone you know. Picture that person's face and imagine him or her receiving hidden blessings. Don't be surprised if your loved one calls you out of the blue. Send that person a small gift when you get a chance.

- **Blissful Silence.** Shut down your computer and switch off the power strip under your desk. Power down your phone and remove the SIM card. Unplug your landline. Commit to observing two hours without any technological interruptions. Use a portion of the time for meditation and the rest for working on a neglected project. See what it feels like to not be interrupted. Your initial anxiety will give way to a real pleasure—personal time and space. Repeat this exercise when you are in a slump and see what a difference it makes.

Solar Exercise

Find a simple sudoku or chess problem. See how long it takes you to solve it. Record on a scratch piece of paper the number of times your mind wandered to something else. Repeat the same exercise a few times each week and see if your concentration has improved. If your attention was diverted, notice any recurring themes. A pattern of distraction centered around a particular problem or issue indicates something that needs attention. Make some time in your schedule this week to deal with the recurring distraction.

Lunar Exercise

Divide a piece of paper into four quarters, and assign four waking hours to each quarter. Then draw a sketch that depicts how you normally feel during that time of day. You can also use words and phrases if you like to supplement your drawings. This will give you an overall picture of how your day looks. When you have time, repeat the exercise for how you would *like* to feel during each part of the day and draw new pictures to replace the old ones. Put the picture in your meditation space as a visual prayer.

CHAPTER SUMMARY

- Becoming more aware of how you tend to waste time will help you to develop strategies for fixing the problem.
- Boredom stems from avoiding things that you don't want to do and losing sight of your own intrinsic motivation.

- Tasks that may feel good may not be the best ways to spend time, and those that feel tedious can be the most important.
- Making the move to monotasking can be a great relief as you realize that you have more time for the things that you love.

CHAPTER 7

TRANSFORMATION

By now, you've probably seen some signs that your meditation practice is working. The trick now is to keep yourself motivated after the novelty has faded. Following some of the best practices that have worked for others will help.

Turning Points

At this point, you have (hopefully!) done several of the exercises in this book, and you have made a concerted effort to de-clutter your life physically and mentally. You probably had a few times when you felt like an idiot sitting there with your eyes closed, doing nothing. You may have had some relapses where you forgot to meditate for a while.

But you keep coming back. No matter how long the lapse, you return again to that calm center. That's probably because you saw some results. But don't fixate on the results; if you lean on them too much, you will become discouraged. Remember that meditation has a cumulative effect and may not yield instant gratification. Let good results encourage you to stay on the right track, but don't get worried if you hit a plateau or have times when the meditation doesn't seem to make a difference.

Letting Go of the Craziness

One sign that you're making progress in your meditation practice is when something that previously drove you crazy no longer seems to make much of a difference. Maybe your coworkers are gathered in the hallway, talking about how stressed they are. Oddly enough, you don't feel the need to complain, because you don't have anything to complain about. Suddenly the gripes that seemed so serious now seem a little immature.

Even if you think the grievances are genuine, you will now look for positive solutions instead of just grousing in the hallway. Experiences like this signal that your threshold for annoyance has been raised: you are now a stronger and more stable person because you meditate.

It's a Wonderful World

Another sign of progress is that the world seems more beautiful. You'll catch yourself smiling at some dead leaves blowing across a parking lot or at wisps of clouds overhead. The weather will seem more like a companion and less like an adversary. You'll be more patient in crowds, less apt to inwardly (or outwardly) curse other people. More introverted meditators will find themselves talking to strangers, while extroverts will begin to enjoy a respite from words. Signs like these show that you have gained inner flexibility and openness as a result of your practice.

Unexpected Happiness

As you continue your practice, you'll experience surges of positive emotions for no good reason. This will feel quite undeserved, maybe even irresponsible, because the outward conditions of your life won't have changed all that drastically. The big problems will still be there, but you will have gained a new perspective on them. You will give yourself permission to laugh more and be happy despite the fact that you don't live in a perfect world and you don't have a perfect life. Perfection itself will come to seem oppressive, and you will jettison this particularly unforgiving standard against which to judge your life. You will begin to see what you already have and work with it as the greatest of riches.

One with the World

Meditation helps you sense your kinship with all things, living and nonliving. As you see that the rigid boundaries separating yourself from the outside world are illusions, you'll feel a greater sense of empathy. You will try to tread more lightly on the earth and do whatever you can to minimize suffering. You won't look at yourself as more deserving or better than any other creature. This new sense of connectedness may feel like a difficult burden at times as you see so many instances of cruelty in the world, but it will also make you feel less solitary as you realize you have family members that you never knew you had.

You Are Responsible for You

As your practice deepens and becomes more regular, you begin to take a greater ownership of your own well-being. Rather than blaming all of your problems on circumstances or other people, you look for ways to improve your own life through positive action. You de-emphasize your old victim/martyr self and live into a new, powerful self that makes things happen on your own behalf.

As you claim your own emotional life as well as the management of your own time, space, and attention, other challenges seem less daunting. The difficulty level of your life has been lowered. You will feel like facing the world again, as though you really can make things better for yourself and others.

Distraction-Free Work

As the entire premise of this book promises, meditation will help you work without distraction for greater periods of time, owing to greater concentration and improved mood. Your work no longer seems like endless tedium but holds small joys of its own. You take a pride in your work that you haven't found in years and no longer have to struggle to muster the energy to get going. Coworkers notice a sense of vigor about you and wonder where you get it. When everyone else seems snowed under with busyness, you escape relatively unscathed. You begin to defeat procrastination and start on projects weeks or months in advance.

The Many Faces of You

As your meditation shows you how ephemeral thoughts and feelings are, you start to explore hidden facets of your personality. Your personality seems more like a tool in your hands than something immutable, and you feel free to edit aspects of your self-presentation that aren't working very well. Spontaneous, artistic types become more regimented, and highly structured individuals experience more freedom. You may find yourself behaving uncharacteristically, but this will be fun rather than frightening. You begin to have a sense that you are not wedded to the past but can be whoever you want to be. You become bolder, more innovative and more willing to take risks.

You may not experience all of these changes—and you may experience others not mentioned here. Don't pressure yourself or force any of these changes to happen. They will come with time as you become more rooted in spiritual practice and transform your point of view on the world.

Growing Pains

You may experience some growing pains as you notice parts of yourself that aren't that flattering or venture down unfamiliar paths. Some trepidation is a normal part of the process. Don't force yourself to do something that you aren't ready for. Keep two things in mind: you only have today, and you have all the time in the world. Anxiety can be a powerful motivator, but it can also poison your life. Be grateful for the changes that have come into your life, but also be grateful for who you are at this moment.

If you have yet to see any changes as a result of meditation, it just may not be the right timing for you. You may have a severe case of burnout, you may have skeptical doubts, or you might have substance abuse or other problems that need attention. Clearing up these issues will help. Remember that meditation is best used as part of an overall program of self-care, including all aspects of psychological and physical well-being. If you just can't get on board with meditation now, the seed that you have planted by reading this book may one day produce fruit in the form of an active practice. No effort, no matter how small, ever goes unrewarded, and you may be accomplishing more than you think.

Best Practices

While you can't fail at meditation—there's no failure, just delay—
you can do certain things now to save you years' worth of time in
your personal development. Let's take a look at some best practices
that will ensure your success:

- Meditators who have two "anchor" sessions lasting fifteen to
  twenty minutes, one in the morning hours and one in the evening hours, are more likely to stick with the practice and take
  shorter meditation breaks during the day. Optimally, these
  breaks occur at the same place and time, but this is not strictly
  necessary.
- Meditators who incorporate deep breathing into their practice see more results than those who depend on visualization or mindfulness alone. Deep breathing has physiological
  effects that complement other forms of meditation. Seeing
  early results makes it more likely that you will stick with the
  practice, and because deep breathing exercises are easy to do,
  they can help you feel more immediately rewarded for your
  efforts.
- Meditators who see their spiritual practice as part of an overall
  program of well-being are more likely to continue meditating.
  This means eating a good diet, exercising, and getting regular
  physical and mental health checkups.
- Meditators who find a community of like-minded individuals
  are more likely to continue with the practice. A community
  could be anything from an online chat room to a temple to a
  yoga class.

- Meditators who keep learning and growing in their spiritual lives are less inclined to drop the practice. You may find it useful to settle on a particular style or school of meditation and receive formal instruction. When you are at the right time in your practice, a teacher will appear who will guide you further down the path. In the meantime, reading books and going to workshops will help keep the practice lively and interesting.
- Monotasking and meditation work better together than either technique works alone. When paired, these two strategies have a multiplying effect, one working from the inside and the other from the outside. By combining these approaches, you avoid one of the common pitfalls of spiritual practice, which is a tendency to divide the world between the sacred and the profane. Work will be uplifted when the inner self is allowed to participate more fully in it.

Mindfulness Mantras

Think of those situations in your life where you feel timid, confused, worried, or powerless. Breathe deeply and imagine your breath energizing those troubled areas. Give yourself to greater responsibility and freedom, for these two qualities are two sides of the same coin. See yourself easily moving beyond difficulties, expanding your horizons, and accessing your spontaneous intuition. Close with the prayer, "Aum, shanti, shanti, shanti. Aum, peace, peace, peace." When you open your eyes, find three ways to improve a negative situation in your life. Other mindfulness meditations or prayers to aid you:

Perfect Love

Take a minute to put down whatever you are doing. Symbolically turn off your computer monitor or place any papers face down. Repeat slowly and deliberately, "Perfect love casts out fear." Relax the muscles of your face, especially your brow. Allow the corners of your mouth to turn upward in a smile. Let go of any resistance to the words and believe in them with all of your might. When you return to the everyday world, allow the prayer to echo in your head.

Om

Om (A-U-M) is the primal sound, the sound of the universe as it goes through its threefold process of creation, preservation, and destruction. Practice saying the "om" to yourself. If you are alone, say it out loud, lengthening the syllable as the word resonates in your chest, throat, and head. If you are around other people, repeat it mentally. As you go throughout your day, see if you can hear the "om" on the wind, in the babble of conversation, or in the whirring of a computer.

Five-Minute Exercises

These exercises can provide a needed break in a busy day or a way to wind down upon coming home or before bed. You will learn to relax body, mind, and spirit through these simple techniques.

Full-Body Relaxation

When you have a little bit of privacy, lie down flat on the floor with your arms slightly out from the sides of your body, with your feet a shoulder-width apart. Feel your body sinking into the floor.

Allow your tongue to fall back in your mouth and even picture your eyeballs sinking further into your skull. Then begin systematically relaxing each part of your body. Say to yourself, "I relax my feet. My feet are totally relaxed. I relax my calves and thighs. My calves and thighs are totally relaxed. I relax my stomach and lower back. My stomach and lower back are totally relaxed. I relax my chest and upper back. My chest and my upper back are totally relaxed. I relax my arms and my shoulders. My arms and my shoulders are totally relaxed. I relax my neck. My neck is totally relaxed. I relax my face. My face is totally relaxed." If any spots of tension remain, breathe deeply into them. Picture yourself surrounded by the stars of the night sky. Remain in this dark space for the remainder of the time. When you are done, slowly open your eyes, roll onto your side, and come to a sitting position. Say a prayer of gratitude before returning to the day.

The Cave of the Heart

Sit up straight, either cross-legged on the floor or in a chair with your feet on the floor. Begin by breathing deeply, concentrating your awareness between the eyes. When you have entered fully into a rhythm of deep breathing, observe your internal space, the darkness before your eyes. You may see subtle lights, like electric sparks floating around. You may see mental formations like words and images, or you may see the outlines of your body or the room in which you are sitting.

Gradually move your center of awareness downward along your spinal column, until it rests in the center of your chest. This may be a little difficult, because we think of the head as the seat of consciousness. With a little effort, you should be able to remain in the chest region. Now begin to see this space. You may sense darkness, or you may visualize your heart and lungs expanding and contracting.

Now allow this area to fill with a white light tinged with violet. Picture this light as a countervailing force against the words and images in your head, just as the sun breaks through rain clouds after a storm. Make this inner vision stronger, until the light is extremely powerful. After the visualization is established, stop trying to consciously produce it. Go back to simply observing. Realize that light and darkness are not opposites but part and parcel of the same reality. Know that you carry a shrine with you wherever you go, in the cave of the heart.

Ten-Minute Exercises

These prayers and mantras are time-honored phrases to bring you into a more peaceful frame of mind. They easily remove mental clutter and focus your attention. Once memorized, which happens easily, these sayings accompany you everywhere and can be welcome friends in good and bad times.

Chanting

Choose one of the following prayers or mantras and repeat it 108 times, silently or aloud. If you have time left at the end, allow the feeling of the words to reverberate silently. Work on amplifying the effects of the prayer so that you become one with it. Use a mala (a string of 108 beads made from *rudraksha seeds, tulasi* (holy basil), or gemstones, a Western rosary (Roman Catholic, five decade, or Orthodox prayer rope, 33 or 100 knots) to count the prayers, or make hash marks on a piece of paper. Some meditation websites also sell mantra counters that can be useful.

- *Aum gam ganapataye namah.* Pronounced "om gahm gana pata *yeh* nama *hah*." This prayer to Ganesha, the Hindu elephant-god and remover of all obstacles, bestows both worldly and spiritual success. As you repeat the mantra, reflect on some of Ganesha's more inward qualities: he is absorbed in meditation, ever-patient, kind, and loving. You may also choose to reflect on his outward qualities. He is a fierce warrior, filled with power, a scourge to his enemies. You can also think about the qualities of an actual elephant—the famed memories of these creatures, as well as their ability to travel thousands of miles without tiring.

- *Aum shring hring kleeng mahalakshmi namah.* Pronounced "om shring/shreem, hring kling maha luck/lahk shmi nama *hah*." This prayer praises and asks the help of Lakshmi, great goddess of wealth, beauty, and wisdom and wife of Vishnu, the god of preservation. The mystical syllables at the beginning contain Lakshmi's seed sound, *shring*, the sound that encapsulates her nature, and syllables that pray for increase in insight. The syllables also recall the sound of falling coins, one of the goddess's hallmarks. Think of her filling the spaces of your life with beauty as you give her thanks and praise. Think of material wealth having its source in creation itself, the original wealth.

- *Shema Yisrael Adonai Eloheinu Adonai Echad.* Pronounced "shem-ah yees-ra-el a-don-ai el-o-hi-noo e-had." Translated, this means, "Hear Oh Israel, the Lord is our God, the Lord is

One." This phrase is the beginning of the foundational prayer of Judaism that is important for Christianity and Islam as well. Focus on the concept of "hear" and allow it to open your inner and outer ears, tuning you in to the world. As you move to the second part of the prayer, think about the diversity of things and appearances in the world and reflect on their commonality. You may choose to think of this God as an all-pervading divine essence or as energy or Being. If you are more scientifically minded, think about the Big Bang or the whorl of a galaxy. Realize that this unseen One lies in your own heart as well.

- *Faith, hope, and love abide, but the greatest of these is love.* This saying from 1 Corinthians is used in many Christian wedding ceremonies and worship services. As you say these words, try to bring these qualities into your own heart and mind. Direct faith, hope, and love toward the people and situations in your life as you say the prayer. Think of some ways that you may have held back from exercising them due to a sense of futility or powerlessness. Resolve to do your utmost to love others and to make the world a better place.

- *I take refuge in the Buddha, the Dharma, and the Sangha.* The Buddha is, of course, the Enlightened One who encouraged his followers to see the impermanence of all things and follow the Middle Way. The Dharma is the eternal word or law that all actions produce effects, good or bad, and also refers to the spiritual teachings of Buddhism. The Sangha is the community of fellow-seekers treading the same path. This triple jewel will protect you in times of confusion and anxiety.

- *Aum Mani Padme Hum*. Pronounced "Om Mani Pahd *may* Hmmm." It means "Behold the Jewel in the Lotus." As you say this famous Buddhist mantra, picture a lotus flower, resplendent with color and light, blooming in the cave of your heart. At the center of the lotus is a large jewel or diamond, perfectly clear and brilliant. Imagine your heart opening to receive the world, welcoming all beings with infinite compassion.

Solar Exercise

Count the number of ads you see or hear in a day. Include billboards, packaging, advertisements (print, radio, TV, or online), product placement, sponsorships, and author/producer interviews. The sheer number of ads will surprise you, and you may find that you forget to count them. You may even view ads without even realizing that you are doing it. After completing the exercise, try to reduce your exposure to advertising and be conscious about how the ads affect your mental and emotional (not to mention, financial) life.

Lunar Exercise

Find a favorite musical recording, preferably something without too many words. In a comfortable chair, listen to the music through headphones. Listen to the music without thinking about other things. How easy did you find it to only listen to music? The next day, try meditating without music for five minutes. Then put on the headphones and try again. Did you notice a difference after meditating?

CHAPTER SUMMARY

- After getting established in a regular routine of meditation, you experience bursts of happiness, you can work for longer periods without distraction, and you come to know yourself better.
- To keep yourself going for the long haul, find a community of like-minded people, make a plan for overall health, and incorporate deep breathing into your practice.
- Mantra practice can be an easy way to focus your mind and a portable way to meditate wherever you are.

PART III

FOCUSING IN PRACTICE

CHAPTER 8

FOCUSING ON THE HEART

Through mythological and scientific insights, you can explore the heart center, a potent site of creative transformation. Understanding the ethics of the heart shows you how to balance your emotions with rational thought and vice versa. Recognizing the wisdom of the heart shows you how to connect with others and with the cosmos.

The Heart as the Seat of Emotion

In ancient cultures around the world—from Greece and Rome to India and Egypt to the Americas to China—the heart was considered the origin of affection, emotion, and passion. It was often viewed as the seat of the soul and of personhood.

While modern medicine has taught us the physical purpose of the heart, and that our emotions arise from our brains, we still think of the heart as the place where our emotions live. We speak of having a broken heart, or a crooked one; a heart bursting with joy or enflamed with love or anger.

"The heart has its reasons which reason knows not of."

—BLAISE PASCAL

The Undivided Heart

The heart has undergone something of a demotion in recent times; we might think of it as simply a pump for the blood and nothing more. We know that we need to watch our intake of cholesterol to help our hearts keep beating, but the intelligence of the heart has been forgotten. Or we divide our understanding of the heart into two compartments: the heart of love songs and the heart of medical science.

But this division isn't necessary. After all, the heart is connected to the brainstem through a network of nerves; the brainstem is, in turn, connected to the intellect. In situations of emotional upset, the heart does, indeed, beat faster, which gives us that sinking or aching feeling in the chest. And the person who can glide past the troubles of life, who has a clean conscience, a "good heart," will, indeed, live longer on average, because a calm person has a heart that beats slower, a heart that is younger. And the heart, viewed as a seat of life by cultures around the world, does give life to the body by supplying the cells with oxygen and nutrition.

World Heart Traditions

While the ancient wisdom might be viewed as metaphorical today, metaphors always have some truth behind them. We would do well to think of the heart as having an intelligence of its own and to pay attention to the heart in the practice of meditation. We can learn a lot from heart practices around the world.

The Sacred Heart

Some of the most famous heart images are the sacred heart iconography of Jesus and Mary, products of the Roman Catholic devotional tradition. In the artworks related to the devotion, the heart appears ringed with a crown of thorns, pierced with a spear or sword, and radiating sunlight or flames. Jesus or Mary gestures toward the exposed heart, seeming to invite the viewer inside.

Indeed, while Protestants tend to speak of inviting Jesus into the heart, Catholic mysticism focuses on entering into the heart of Jesus or Mary. By reflecting on the wounds of Christ, the devotee participates in the story of the passion, which unites the divine and the human in the drama of suffering and forgiveness. The Sacred Heart is called by such titles as a "glowing furnace of charity" and the "house of God and gate of heaven." The person who meditates on the Sacred Heart also meditates on the Eucharist and gains both heavenly merit and material sufficiency.

The Divine Powers

In the Jewish mystical tradition of Kabbalah, derived from intense study of the Hebrew scriptures, the ten *sefirot*, or enumerations of the divine powers, are located on the "tree of life" which correspond to the parts of the human body and to the universe itself. This idea traces back to Paracelsus, who said that the body is a microcosm of the universe, containing within it all of the materials and potentials of the external world.

In Kabbalah, the heart lies in the central *sefirah,* called *Tif'eret,* which stands for both beauty and balance. Here lies the creative tension between love and judgment, good and evil. Without the balance of these forces, the universe could not exist at all, because it would be destroyed by the wrath of God or float away in ethereal goodness. As the trunk of the tree of all existence, *Tif'eret* unites the upward reaching, mystical nature with the earthward, practical nature as well as left and right, inside and outside, male and female, Dionysian and Apollonian. Without formally studying Kabbalah, we can still gain the inspiration from this wisdom tradition to always balance our spiritual natures with worldly concerns, to temper our anger with compassion, to wed masculine and feminine qualities.

Advanced Meditation Suggestion

Try meditating in silence for thirty minutes in the morning. Carry that interior silence throughout the day. Each time you are having a conversation with yourself, go back to a listening, receptive attitude. If you forget that you are doing the exercise and go back to your ordinary consciousness, don't worry. Try again the next day.

The Heart Chakra

In the Indian traditions of *ayurveda* (Hindu medicine) and *kundalini* (energy practice), the *anahata*, or heart chakra (wheel or center of energy), also has aspects of balance. The "fourth chakra" resides between three chakras below and three above, and between the *ida* (left, lunar, and feminine) and *pingala* (right, solar, and masculine) currents of the body. The person who has brought energy into the fourth chakra will begin to transcend passion and live a spiritual life, going beyond the limitations of the present situation to see the larger picture. This chakra is symbolized by a twelve-petaled lotus or the color green, and is called *the chakra of direct cognition*, because the heart knows through illumination and insight rather than conscious mental effort. Opening the heart chakra through breath control and meditation allows the spiritual seeker to advance more rapidly on the path.

Ethics of the Heart

Our emotions can be powerful guides, leading the way before the rational mind catches up, but they can be misleading ones as well. Just as being overly rational can lead to destructive behaviors, being overly emotional can be equally destructive. Guilt feelings can be destructive, leading to unhealthy behaviors and even mental health issues. Romantic feelings can be used to justify abusive relationships or infidelity. So how do we reconcile the heart's wisdom with the heart's waywardness?

The mind is not above or better than the heart; neither is the heart above or better than the mind. Imagine the heart as just a part of the mind—or the mind as just a part of the heart. Caring about something in an emotional way can lead to an intellectual engagement, as when someone who cares about wetlands becomes a conservation biologist or an animal lover becomes a veterinarian. You don't learn about the candidates in an election unless you feel like your vote might make a difference; you know all about your favorite city but many others are indistinguishable to you.

The Origin of Ethical Behavior

Ethics, derived from the Greek word for "habit," refers to the proper standard of action, the way to act that leads to happiness and the good life for all. Oftentimes people think that correct action comes from following the dictates of conscience or the prescriptions of religion.

Differences immediately arise however, about what actions are appropriate and which ones are not. Apparently we each have a conscience that speaks a different language, and religion can't be relied upon to furnish secure foundations, since it has often been used to sanction questionable behavior. The second any dispute arises, we have need of ethics, which can be defined as formal reflection on the right way to live.

A complete ethical treatise is beyond the scope of this book, but some discussion of ethics is appropriate, because living in harmony with other people and the natural environment is a necessary prerequisite to the practice of meditation. It will do no good trying to get our heads right if we haven't gotten our lives right. We need not be perfect before beginning the practice of meditation, otherwise we would never begin, but we should be headed in the right direction or, at a bare minimum, have a sincere wish to do so.

We should strive to reduce the harm that our lives cause to other people, to animals, and to the earth, and we should also seek to benefit the world, so that it will be improved by our having been here. Life will present us with many gray areas, where the right course of action is not clear cut. It is useful to sketch out a few general observations in order to make the path not clear, perhaps, but a little easier to find. We begin by looking closer at the relationship between the feelings and the mind.

Your Mind's Connection to Your Emotions

Your mind takes its cues from your emotions. So we can say that the heart is the leading edge of the mind. Rational processes can augment or overturn what your heart says. Rationality, alone, however, doesn't lead to ethical behavior; that requires the involvement of the heart. Many atrocities in world history have been perfectly rational—perversely so—and the same holds true today. Indigenous people are displaced and killed to build hydroelectric dams and graze cattle; we spend billions on weapons while our schools fail; and we have money for new clothes and gadgets but not for charitable organizations. None of this is irrational, exactly—it's just misplaced rationality, what we call *rationalization*. The mind vetoes the heart.

Becoming Deeply Ethical

Many people display acceptable behavior: they don't hit other people, they pay their taxes, and they don't steal from the grocery store. But to become more deeply ethical, living in such a way as to benefit the world rather than just holding to social acceptability or permissible action, you have to have three things:

1. To be truly ethical, as opposed to just following social convention, you need a mentor or a role model. You need someone to model your life after, someone who will stretch you to become greater than your limited self-concept. It could be any number of world-changing leaders: Mother Teresa, Dietrich Bonhoeffer, Dorothy Day, Martin Luther King, Jr., Helen and Scott Nearing, Mahatma Gandhi, or Ramana Maharshi. A personal mentor can work as well: school teachers, best friends, parents, and grandparents.

Don't put these heroes, well-known or obscure, up on a pedestal so that they are unapproachable. Even Jesus and the Buddha were people just like you, who had good days and bad days, who might have disappeared into the dust-bin of history. While you might not become exactly like your personal luminaries, you should let them influence and shape you. Look upon them as coaches in the game of life, people who can help you become your very best, even if they are dead and gone. Don't think of their stories and teachings as relics from the past but as vibrant portals into the deepest meanings of your life.

2. A truly ethical life requires you to follow an ethical tradition. Such traditions encourage you to transcend yourself and live for a deeper purpose, beyond the consumer materialism and other shallow values of contemporary society. This does not mean you should follow these ethical traditions rigidly or robotically, but to take what you find valuable and jettison the rest. Tradition should help you to live your life with purpose and commitment but should not tie you to outmoded beliefs or lead you to condemn others.

3. An ethical life lies in finding and expressing your own unique personality and insights. You have unique ethical impulses—things that you are called to do that may not be asked of anyone else. Your unique, personal ethic could be expressed through music or artwork, through social action, or through your relationships. You have to discover these pathways for yourself, looking at what situations in your life call you to action. Ask what moves you, what makes you want to act. Then take small steps toward that vision. You

don't need to quit your job or sell your possessions. Just tap into those impulses in your heart and make them a reality, one step at a time.

Heart Wisdom

With this ethical framework in place, we can turn to the heart as a gateway of wisdom. The heart can be an instruction where words fail, a guide where no principles can go.

Opening Your Heart to the Divine

By opening your heart to the divine realm, you will invite wisdom into your life. If you follow a specific religion, you can view the heart as a portal that God (or the gods) can use to enter your life. Your heart becomes the place where this higher power lives. You can visualize this divinity in whatever way coincides with your religious tradition: a light, a dove, a god or goddess, Jesus or the Prophet, the Ark of the Covenant, or the Holy of Holies. If you're an atheist or agnostic, you can invite the wisdom of nature into your heart. The symbols you visualize can be a fire or a still body of water. Or, you can meditate on qualities like peace, patience, or love, and invite these higher realities into your heart. As you meditate, open your heart to the reality that you want to bring into your life. The heart center will then make that reality manifest in thought and finally in action.

Open Your Heart to the Cosmos

As you meditate on the heart center, you may first find there the people, places, and things that you already care about. You may hold your family and friends in your heart, or your hometown, or some woods where you played as a child. This is a very good place to begin—indeed, where else can you begin except with the familiar? But to open your heart to the cosmos, you have to move beyond the familiar. Open up your circle to include strangers, both those nearby and those in faraway countries, especially places experiencing war or natural- or human-caused disasters. Hold in your heart prisoners of conscience and just plain prisoners and send forth the intention that they receive humane treatment and fair trials.

Then move to the animal kingdom and hold in your heart. Send forth your well wishes to all creatures, that they may have sufficient habitat, food, and clean water. Then reflect on trees and plants, appreciating their good qualities and the way they provide for you (and for all of us). Ask (God, the gods, the universe, the cosmic forces, the Tao, the Buddha, or fill in the blank) that the forests be preserved from destruction and that all plant species flourish.

Finally reflect on the earth, the stars, the planets—the entire cosmos. Be mindful of your small place within the universe and keep the intention of not overstepping your bounds.

All of these intentions should take place within your heart center. You can visualize this in the anatomically correct fashion or stylized into a Valentine's Day heart. You can picture it as a box, a room, a temple, or other concrete space. Superimpose images of the people, creatures, and things that you are reflecting on and thinking about.

"The kingdom of God is within you."

—JESUS

Putting Thoughts Into Action

You can't act on good thoughts if you don't have them to act on. Meditation helps you generate those positive thoughts. After meditation is over, you can then take concrete actions that make your spiritual vision a reality.

Life and thought mutually influence one another and magnify one another. Positive thoughts lead to positive actions, and negative thoughts lead to negative actions.

In the Hindu and Buddhist traditions, among others, thought is considered a kind of action (*karma*) and is not viewed as separate just because it does not take place in the physical world. Western traditions have variants of this same idea, and modern psychology affirms that our thoughts shape our emotional reactions, which in turn shape our responses.

If we can condition ourselves to be negative, cynical, and sarcastic, we can also condition ourselves to be optimistic, bold, and generous.

Your Heart as a Physical Entity

The heart plays a crucial role in circulation and respiration, as it pumps day in and day out to supply each and every cell with necessary nutrients and oxygen. The body doesn't exist in a vacuum, though. After all, what good would it do to have lungs if the world had no air to breathe? What good would it do to have a brain without a world to perceive? Everything is intimately interconnected.

In meditation, you become aware of the constant beating of your heart, the flow of blood in your arteries and veins. This reminds you of the greater truth that everything is in flux, in circulation—and interconnected. Think of all sorts of ebbs and flows: life and death, creation and destruction, the waxing and waning of the moon, and the cycle of the seasons.

The heart reminds you that you are a terrestrial mammal, dependent upon your environment and others for your life and livelihood. Remember the heart and think about its steady presence, the drumbeat of existence.

Heart as Calm Anchor

Meditating on the heart center can help to soothe troubled emotional states. Life is full of disappointments and upsets, obstacles and transitions, and even the most enlightened souls will experience anguish. No matter how good you are at problem solving or spiritual discipline, you can't make pain and suffering go away. Hurting is a fact of life, one that you should not attempt to shed.

You can, however, manage your responses to events. The purpose isn't to get rid of suffering, but to deal with it in the most honest and direct way. Reflecting on the heart center can help you manage your response to pain. Notice that even beneath the most serious upset, your heart goes on beating as before.

Hear blood rushing in your ears and feel it pulsing in your neck. You may be able to feel it in your legs and fingertips. Listen to this steady pulsing, which serves as a reminder that you are still alive. The pains of life prove that you are here, that you have lived and continue to live, and the beating of your heart conveys the message that your life is not over and that the story continues.

Take refuge here in your heart and make it your home: the storms will pass, and you will emerge from them wiser and stronger.

One-Minute Exercises

These exercises will help you to become more aware of the heart center and use it to cultivate compassion. You will move from a view of the heart as a mechanical pump for blood to a luminous center for healing and grace.

A Heart Intention

Stand comfortably and close your eyes. Repeat the following intention: "My heart, take in the whole world. My heart, balance my turbulent emotions. My heart, grow more loving and wise. Sacred heart, fill me with your radiance." As you say the intention, center your awareness in your chest and picture your heart as an ever-expanding chamber. How you visualize the heart is up to you—as an anatomical model, as a temple, as a cave, as a treasure chest, or whatever you wish.

Heart Awareness

Sit very still and quiet and try to sense your heart beating in your chest. If you can't feel it in your chest, try paying attention to your neck and head. With practice, you should be able to feel your pulse from the inside, without using your fingertips. You may also hear the blood rushing in your ears; it sounds like a distant running river. Once you sense your heartbeat and your rushing blood, take some time to quietly observe.

Five-Minute Exercises

If you have a few extra minutes, these five-minute exercises can help you do some brief meditation and create a sense of grounding and centeredness.

An Intention for Connectedness

Repeat the intention twenty-seven times, counting on beads or your fingertips: "My heart, take in the whole world. My heart, balance my turbulent emotions. My heart, grow more loving and wise. Sacred heart, fill me with your radiance."

As you repeat the intention, picture your heart expanding and becoming more porous. The outlines of your body also expand and become porous, translucent. Once you are established in the intention and your breathing has slowed, you may wish to reflect on specific intentions. Picture friends and acquaintances who may be having a hard time right now, troubled spots on the global stage, or any particularly difficult issues in your life. Don't go overboard with the internal dialogue. Focus on images of who and what you want to see healed, but the words of the intention itself should take center stage. For a twenty-minute exercise, make 108 repetitions of the prayer.

Grandmother's Kitchen

For some people, grandparents are a source of unconditional love. Think of your grandmother in a particularly good moment, one of those times when you felt loved and supported. It doesn't matter if your grandparents have passed away; the important thing is to capture that feeling. Imagine yourself sitting at the kitchen table with her on her best behavior. Physical details will help too, like what kind of table did she have in her kitchen? What snacks did she serve you? What phrases did she use most often? You can now erase all of the bad qualities your grandmother may have had. Forget about any negative political beliefs or prejudices and concentrate on her love. Now simply tell her in your mind anything that might be bothering you, any troubles that you want to let go. Then listen quietly and see if you get a response. You may find yourself entering into a conversation with her. If you can't make it happen, don't worry. Just remember what it felt like to be loved unconditionally.

Ten-Minute Exercise: Sacred Wounds

This exercise helps to release past hurts that may prevent you from expressing your full potential. You may have some traumatic experiences that have always lingered in the shadows, because you were not capable of releasing them. These old wounds may make you overly cautious in some areas or prevent you from developing emotional connections with others. As you go through this exercise, be gentle with yourself. Don't try to force yourself to let go of something before you are ready.

Bring awareness to your heart center through deep breathing and close observation. Feel your heart beating in your head, the rush of blood through your arteries and veins. See how the heart nourishes and enlivens your whole body. See it not only as an organ, but as the essence of yourself, spreading beneficent energy to your whole self: body, mind, and spirit. Now go into a diligent listening mode. Ask your heart to reveal its wounds to you, the ways it has been hurt in the past that prevent your growth from going forward. Don't force the issue. If nothing comes to you, do not try to make the experience happen. You can always try again later.

Some scene from your past may appear in your mind's eye: a coworker who criticized you, a former lover who left you, a public embarrassment of some kind. Be prepared for something unexpected that you buried deep inside. Simply notice this wound from the past and acknowledge it. That may be as far as the exercise goes for now.

If you feel ready (and only if you feel ready), speak into that wound. Say to your past hurt, "I am ready to let you go. I forgive those who were responsible, I forgive myself, and I am ready to turn this wound into a source of strength." Picture the same radiant energy that pulses throughout your body washing over your wounded heart.

When you are finished with the exercise, your heart will still bear its wounds, but the scars will be healed to a greater degree than they were before. Particularly deep wounds may require multiple sessions. The important thing is to not force the issue—let your heart progress as it will. Deep breathing and visualization work will help. As you realize your own boundless power (which is nothing other than that which keeps the universe in existence), the hurts of the past will seem less and less consequential. You may never forget what has happened to you in the past (and you probably shouldn't), but those past events will cease to have a strong hold on you.

Solar Exercise

Fill a glass of water to the brim and balance it on one open palm (without wrapping your fingers around the glass). See how long you can hold it without spilling a drop. Notice any thoughts that form and see if they help or harm the process.

Switch hands and try it again. If you can do this without any problem, try walking the glass of water around the house. See if you can bring this same concentration to bear on other parts of your life.

Lunar Exercise

With some finger paints and a big tablet of craft paper, sit down and finger paint a landscape, a bowl of fruit, or anything else that suits your fancy.

Do you feel ridiculous finger painting? What resistance arises in your mind? Do you feel the need to get it right? Just enjoy the squish of the paints on your fingers, the dance of colors across the page, and the grade school nostalgia.

CHAPTER SUMMARY

- The heart chakra or heart center balances turbulent emotions and quells rational thought.
- Living an ethical life, a prerequisite for meditation, requires balancing the heart (intuition and emotion) with the head (rationality and planning).
- To live a more deeply ethical life, find a role model, follow an ethical tradition, and express your own uniqueness.
- The physical, beating heart reminds us of the cyclical nature of existence and the fragility of life.

CHAPTER 9

FOCUSING ON THE BODY

Your body is a portal to higher consciousness. You can use meditation to deal with chronic pain and illness and learn a few simple yoga postures to improve your practice.

Your Body's Memory

Your body holds a record of everything that happens to you. Everyone has a scar story, a broken leg story, an appendicitis story. Our bodies are like physical memories, artifacts of times past. This also explains why people get tattoos, piercings, and plastic surgery: we view our bodies as extensions of our identities, as ways of expressing ourselves.

Your body also carries your life's labor, as manifested in back and neck pain, sore arms and legs, and carpal tunnel syndrome. Your personality, too, is carried in your body, particularly in the spine. Leading with your chest suggests confidence, while slouching can mean fatigue or low self-esteem. Highly outgoing people tend to be more expressive with their hands and leave their body posture open, while introverts are less animated and keep their body posture closed. You probably lie somewhere in between these extremes, but your personality can still be read in your limbs, in your unique tics and idiosyncrasies.

Your body is your mind externalized, and your mind is your body internalized. You can use your body, then, to transform your mind. Traditional sciences show how to use the body for spiritual practice. As a meditator, you can tap into those traditions to take your mind to a higher level.

Exploring Chinese and Indian Traditional Sciences

While getting into a detailed discussion of traditional sciences is beyond the scope of this book, looking at some general principles they share can help you in your meditation practice.

Traditional Chinese and Indian sciences, like *chi gong* and *ayurveda*, recognize that natural energies flow through the body along specific pathways and can be used to cure disease and open the mind to its full potential. Both the Chinese and Indian systems have physical exercises designed to increase physical stamina and bring energy into the body, and both have practices of herbal medicine and acupuncture/acupressure related to energy points in the body. Both have detailed maps of these energy points (meridians or *nadis*) that the practitioner can use to affect healing.

Called *chi* in the Taoist and Buddhist traditions and *prana* in the Hindu tradition, this energy is closely related to the breath but is not synonymous with *breath*. It might better be called *life force*. This life force can be strengthened through the practice of yoga, a broad term that includes various Indian and Asian systems of exercise. Meditators can benefit greatly from the practice of yoga, tai chi, martial arts, and other body disciplines.

In this chapter, we'll talk about a few exercises from these disciplines, but consider exploring them further on your own. To become aware of prana notice the changes that take place in your body as you meditate:

- Sweat may bead on your forehead when you meditate, especially when you do intensive breath work.
- Goose bumps may form on your arms, which indicates a shift in your body's electrical system.
- A warm and tingly sensation may occur in your hands or face.

These changes signal an increase of life energy in your body. According to tradition, increasing your life force brings longevity and health.

Sensing Auras

Your body has an electrical field surrounding it, which you may be able to sense or see as your own aura. You may not be able to see the multicolored, almond-shaped light display touted by psychics and gurus as extending inches or even feet around the body, but you can observe *something* around the edges of your skin.

To practice, place one of your hands against a light-colored wall. You will see a slight difference in the light just beyond your fingertips, kind of like a mirage, which may have subtle coloration. Imagine this phenomenon growing more brilliant, and you have the aura.

Sensing Life Energy in the World

To sense prana in nature, you need only be attuned to your surroundings. After deep meditation, you may sense an intensely beautiful, roiling energy around stones and plants. Or you may simply have the feeling that a place is different somehow, that you have a sudden sense of well-being. This is an indicator that you have found a good spot for meditation, because the prana in that spot is readily accessible.

You may also notice that it is easier to meditate around monasteries and ashrams, because you physically benefit from the prana of the souls of monastics. The space itself becomes charged with spiritual energy, and just walking onto the grounds of a temple where sincere worship takes place alters the body's makeup. Making a pilgrimage to a holy site is another good way to experience the vibrations of that place and of the other worshipers drawn there.

Finding the Spirit Through the Body

Notice also the postures and gestures associated with the religious traditions of the world: bowing, genuflecting, and prostrating. All of these bodily practices are ways of getting at the spirit through the body. In fact, perhaps it's best to do away with the tired opposition of spirit and flesh altogether. As long as we believe that the material and the spiritual are two separate spheres, we condemn ourselves to a less than satisfactory experience. Think of your body as itself a holy thing, a spiritual entity bringing life and energy into the world. Don't think of "heaven" or "God" as somewhere "out there," think rather that you hold the divine in your own hands, that you are a gate of wisdom and a channel for love and peace.

Think of the places where you live, especially those places where you spend time meditating, as magical lands, as enchanted places where impossible things happen. You may feel silly or childlike doing this, but without a sense of wonder and expectancy, it will be difficult to sustain the effort of meditation until it produces results. Overly rationalizing your experiences will kill them, so give yourself a little free rein for fanciful thinking. You will discover that your childish imaginings can be quite real.

Using Meditation to Heal

The multitasking lifestyle can be punishing on the body. You have probably experienced muscle aches and pains, perhaps chronic headaches and fatigue. You may have other health problems, such as high blood pressure or diabetes. Meditation can help you to relieve these conditions while transitioning into a more sane and healthy lifestyle. You can find relief from physical problems through meditation. It's not a substitute for medical care, but it can be a highly effective complement to it.

You may meditate to get relief from chronic pain, high blood pressure, or another problem. Remember that meditation is part of an overall program of health and well-being that includes exercise and a good diet. Meditation helps you to make these healthy lifestyle choices by augmenting your willpower and overcoming mental blocks. Meditation also physically changes your body's neurochemical makeup—it doesn't just make you *think* you feel better, it does make you feel better. It doesn't just change your psychology—meditation also changes your physical reality. Your blood pressure and blood sugar will go down. Your cholesterol levels will go down. You will have more energy and be able to lose weight more easily. You will get better sleep, which has a host of good health effects. None of this is hocus pocus, but has been verified with hundreds of peer-reviewed scientific studies.

Meditation for Chronic Conditions

When coping with chronic conditions through meditation, start small. Maybe you can only manage one or two minutes at first. That's fine. Begin where you are and build from there.

Within a few weeks, you may able to manage five minutes, and then ten, and then you can start the twice daily, fifteen-to-twenty-minute practice.

But don't stop with meditation alone. Allow the insights that meditation provides to spill over into other aspects of your life. Begin by noticing how many adjustments you have made in your lifestyle to accommodate the diseased state. Obese people may begin to notice themselves taking the electric cart in the supermarket, the elevator at the mall, and the very closest parking spaces. Over time, mobility is lost as the overweight person accommodates to the weight, which grows even more out of control.

The same is true for physical pain: you alter your routine to avoid having pain in, say, your back, perhaps just skipping a few errands in the beginning. Before you know it, you are spending most of the day in bed, perhaps under the influence of pain killers.

The strategy of accommodating to pain and disease does not work. It disempowers you. Gradually your enjoyment in life goes away. You stop seeing friends, wearing nice clothing, or cooking meals for yourself.

The only way to counter the effects of this cycle is to move beyond the pain or illness. Begin returning to the things that you did when you were well, like going out with friends, making time to exercise, or buying new clothes. The same principle applies to depression and other mental illness. Bringing positive habits into your life will help you deal with the illness and perhaps keep it from worsening. It may even heal the illness. As with the mediation itself, start small with these changes. Once you realize that you can do them, add more.

Meditation for Discernment

Meditation helps you to distinguish between a genuinely debilitating condition and one that you only *think* is debilitating. Pain is not a purely physical stimulus but is rather a combination of mental, physical, and social factors. The same pain that would send one person to the emergency room would lead someone else to just reach for the Tylenol. Our responses to pain start with childhood training. If you have parents who do not make a big deal out of their pains and illnesses, you're more likely to have the same minimal response. If your parents were hypochondriacs, you're more likely to have the same need for medical attention.

Your parents aren't the only factors that influence your pain response. Certain sensitive and imaginative people can mentally magnify their pain. If you have a worrying mindset, you may feel pain more acutely.

Social cues suppress or enhance your experience of pain as well. If you're a soldier, you may be expected to be stoic in the face of pain that would make other people faint. If all your friends tell you horrific childbearing stories, you may experience childbirth as more painful and frightening than someone who heard gentler stories.

This conditioning can be partially or completely overcome through meditation. You will still need medical attention, but meditation prevents overdependence on medicine for everyday well-being. It puts you in charge of your own health and well-being.

Meditation to Experience Well-Being

Meditation also gives you a taste of what well-being is like. If you've been unwell for years, you may forget what it's like to want to get out of bed in the morning. You may forget what it's like to have a surplus of energy, enough to do whatever you might want. Feeling sick, tired, and sad might have become normal for you, and your friends and acquaintances might reinforce this belief for you.

As you begin to meditate, small glimpses of wellness will begin to appear in your life, which will give you impetus to change bad habits. The same snowball effect that led to ill health can also be used to reach good health; it's simply the same process in reverse. You make one positive change, like meditating, which leads to another positive change, like exercising, and suddenly your life is revitalized. Of course, it happens as a process of gradual change, but, looking back on several years of this progress, your life will seem totally different from what it was before.

As you read these words, you may have some skeptical resistance. You may find it hard to believe that you could feel well and happy. Perhaps you don't even remember a time when you felt optimistic, self-confident, loved, and loving. Meditation will make a difference. It won't solve your problems, but it will get you started down the right path.

Change Your Thinking to Change Your Body

In much the same way that the rudder of a ship can turn the whole vessel, your thought process governs your whole life. If you think nothing in your life will ever be good enough, then that will be true: nothing in your life will ever be good enough. But if you have a positive outlook, no obstacle will ever be too big for you. Meditation can create and reinforce this positive outlook.

A more positive outlook may even change your body. Pain begins to go away, and you look and feel better. The benefits of meditation will be felt years down the road in the form of an easier transition into old age and fewer major health concerns.

Meditating, exercising, and eating well help your body respond better to conventional medical treatment, and you will not have as many complaints about your mental or physical well-being. You may see physicians more after you begin meditating, but you will be setting the terms of that engagement by seeing medicine as one tool that you have for living a healthy life. When you no longer perceive yourself as a victim of your DNA or your life circumstances, you will naturally begin to play a greater role in your own well-being. You will realize that health is not about merely combating disease but is about doing the things in life that you want to do, about living with vigor and enthusiasm.

If this sounds impossible now, that's okay. You don't have to commit to always being in a good mood or always feeling great. Just commit to the practice. Do the exercises in this book, and let the results come later. You don't need to banish your internal skeptic. Just don't put that skeptic in charge. Pay no more attention to that nay-saying voice than you would to your crazy uncle at Thanksgiving dinner. That negative voice can have a seat at the table, but it's only one voice at the party. As you delve deeper into meditation, the skeptical voice will ring more and more hollow, and you will be much more cautious about listening to it.

What Meditation Can and Cannot Do

Meditation provides a break in the cycle of disease, here defined as any negative health consequences, regardless of whether or not they have manifested as overt symptoms. As discussed above, meditation does, in itself, improve certain health conditions, but it cannot make up for poor lifestyle choices that may outweigh the benefits of meditation. If you eat a lot of fried foods and animal fats, meditation will not be able to compensate for that. Traditionally meditation goes along with a vegetarian diet, which you might consider. If you aren't willing to make that step, reduce your intake of meat. Lower your portion sizes and limit meat consumption to special occasions or only indulge a couple of times a week. If you struggle with weight gain, consider the fact that vegetarians weigh twenty pounds less on average than meat eaters, and vegans weigh twenty pounds less on average than vegetarians who eat dairy and eggs.

Similarly, if you take a lot of toxins into your body, it will reduce the impact of meditation. Alcohol, preservatives, antibiotics, pesticides, and even caffeine all take a toll on the body. Modern diets are punishing on the internal organs, especially the liver and kidneys, as all of these chemicals are filtered. You may not be able to eat an organic diet with only fresh foods, but being more cognizant of what you eat will increase the impact of meditation. For those who smoke, it should go without saying that quitting now reduces future health problems. Meditation cannot make up for the negative impacts of smoking, but it might be able to help you quit.

These lifestyle changes are part and parcel of meditation, because meditation is the science of getting mind, body, and spirit to work together for greater well-being. If some part of your life is out of harmony, it will manifest in negative consequences. Meditation can help you to detect what changes need to be made and give you the strength to make those changes, but it cannot do all of the work. The insights that you gain while sitting in meditation must then be carried forward into action. It is this feedback loop between action and insight that transforms lives. Each time you sit in meditation, commit to acting on any insights that come your way, even if it entails changing some part of yourself or your habits. If you are not willing to change at all, meditation may not do much good.

Meditation may not be able to cure all diseases, but it can be part of a healing approach to life . Some of "miracle stories" are probably frauds, but some of them are the real thing. Medical professionals call it "spontaneous healing" or "spontaneous remission," short for "we have no idea why this happened." Most doctors and nurses have at least a story or two like this during their medical careers. Don't blame yourself or others if the miracle cure doesn't come, though. Maintain an attitude of hopefulness, but recognize that some things are just beyond your control.

At least three things are happening with regard to your health when you meditate. First, meditation is physically altering your body, changing your chemical and nervous makeup. Next, meditation is altering your psychological makeup, which also manifests physically in the body. Third, meditation changes the way that you interact with the world, getting you to make better choices. Any explanation of meditation that does not consider all three of these underestimates the power of meditation. Don't settle for less than these three areas of change: physical well-being, psychological well-being, and active well-being. Where does the spirit fit into all of this? Well, in all three layers. Spiritual well-being is what happens when people live in a harmonious way with themselves, with each other, and with animals and nature.

Yoga Postures and Meditation

Because your mind and your body are interconnected, what you do with your body will make a big difference in your practice of meditation. Yoga makes physical movement into a form of meditation. Yoga energizes all of your body's tissues and opens a pathway to vibrant health and spiritual well-being. Doing a few simple postures every day will make your body more flexible, get rid of aches and pains, and make it easier to practice seated meditation.

Finding a Good Yoga Teacher

It's a good idea to take classes from a qualified teacher in order to learn a basic routine that you can do at home. Look for a teacher who is certified by a national or international body like the Yoga Alliance. Beyond that, find a teacher who sees yoga as part of a tradition of meditation, and not simply as a form of stretching or physical exercise. Each pose should be geared to breathing, and each transition should be accompanied by an inhalation or exhalation: exhalation for closing or folding postures and inhalation for opening or extending postures. A good teacher will guide you through the breathing that goes with each pose and remind you to breathe rather than hold your breath. If you can, find a teacher who incorporates mantras, meditation, and breath control into each class. If you only have gym-based classes oriented towards physical exercise near you, that's fine. You will still gain great benefits from this type of practice. Make sure that the class is challenging, but not to the extent that it feels competitive. At the end of class, your body should feel like it is humming, tired but also energized. If the thought of doing yoga scares you, many centers have classes geared especially for beginners. The teacher will help you to modify any poses that are too difficult and give you guidance on proper technique. People with back or neck problems should avoid any poses that put strain on these areas, including headstand (*shirshasana*) and shoulder stand (*sarvangasana*).

As you do the poses, bring awareness to and be conscious of every movement of your body. Stay in the moment. Breathe into every posture and feel the subtle changes taking place within.

Beginning meditators can benefit from these simple poses.

Standing Forward Bend (*padahastasana*)

This pose is exactly what it sounds like—a forward bend. Reach upward to the sky and straighten your spine while inhaling. Hold for around thirty seconds. While exhaling, fold forward at the hips, so that your chest goes toward your knees. Your knees should be straight (not locked) or slightly bent. Do not bounce or force the motion in a painful way, just let gravity pull your head downward. Hold for thirty seconds, breathing naturally. Repeat two more times.

Sitting Forward Bend (*paschimottanasana*)

Sit on the floor, with your legs extended straight in front of you with knees straight or slightly bent. Reach upward at a moderate pace with both hands toward the sky while inhaling. On the exhale, bend forward, touching or grasping your knees, ankles, or toes (depending on how far you can reach forward). Relax into the forward stretch and hold for thirty seconds or so while breathing normally. Inhale, stretch upward, and repeat two more times.

Head-to-Knee Pose (*janu shirshasana*)

While sitting on the floor, extend your right leg and tuck your left leg into your groin area. While exhaling, bend forward to the right knee and hold for thirty seconds to one minute while breathing normally. Repeat for the left leg. Go through two more rotations for each leg.

Mountain Pose (*tadasana*)

This standing pose is the foundation for all other standing poses and is a good posture for standing meditation. Place your feet together, big toes touching, heels slightly apart. Balance your weight evenly on both feet, with weight distributed across the heels and balls of your feet and your toes. Open your chest by bringing your shoulders down (not up to your ears) and back. Your ribcage will automatically move upward. Move your arms slightly out from your body so that your hands are about six inches away, palms facing forward. Your face should be relaxed, and your head level.

Half Lotus Position (*ardha padmasana*)

Sit on the floor with your legs straightened in front. Bring your left knee up to your chest, with your foot resting on the floor, giving it a good stretch. Release it, letting it fall to the side. Then place your left foot on your right thigh so that your ankle bone is resting on your thigh. Bend your right leg and tuck it around the front, so that it rests on the floor in front of your left leg. You can also do the pose the opposite way, with your right leg resting on your left thigh.

If half lotus is too difficult, simply sit cross-legged. This is a good general pose for meditation and can be held indefinitely.

One-Minute Exercises

These exercises, designed to fit into even the most hectic day imaginable, help take you out of the crunch to regain clarity. All you need is one minute to re-center yourself and gain peace of mind.

Higher Awareness

Stand in mountain pose (*tadasana*), and, after grounding yourself and taking a few deep breaths, repeat the following intention three times: "I am a vehicle for the higher Self, a channel for the divine." Commit yourself to dynamic, inspired activity for the rest of the day.

One, Not Two

While sitting in half lotus, breathe deeply and root yourself into the floor. Close your eyes and picture the boundary between the inside and the outside of your body dissolving. Then picture the boundary between your daily consciousness and the higher Self dissolving. Finally, picture the division between yourself and other beings dissolving. Commit yourself to working for the good of all for the rest of the day.

Five-Minute Exercises

These quick exercises can help you regain your focus by taking a step back instead of forging ahead. A more deliberate approach can help you deal more effectively with obstacles and challenges.

Clearing Obstacles

When your plans aren't coming together, when you're feeling frustrated and ineffective, it's best to take a short break instead of plowing ahead. Sit up straight in your chair, breathe deeply for three cycles, and picture a particular problem clearly in your mind's eye.

If the problem has a lot of emotion attached to it, breathe into the raw emotions in order to soothe and clear them.

Then take a look at the problem and picture it being solved: a friend coming to offer advice, a coworker taking up the slack, last-minute inspiration occurring, a client satisfied with your work. See the work finished in the best possible way, and take some time to enjoy this feeling. Continue breathing deeply and return to work in a calmer and more confident state of mind.

Peaceful Spaces

As the heart is to the body, the shrine is to the home. If you have taken the time to create a meditation space in your home, you will now connect that space to your own heart center. Just as you have tried to manifest peace in your life through meditating on the heart, you manifest peace in your home through your meditation space.

As you breathe deeply, picture a white light radiating from your heart, filling your chest and even extending beyond your skin. Picture this same light radiating from your home shrine, filling your living space with peace and joy. See potential sources of conflict dissolved and problem areas becoming clear. If you have a small sacred space in your office, picture the same beneficial light energy radiating there as well. Realize that your heart and the shrine are one and the same—the shrine is an outward reflection of the heart, the heart an inward reflection of the shrine. When you approach your home this evening, be mindful, prepared to receive grace, peace, and joy. Note how reality conforms to your expectations.

Ten-Minute Monotask

This exercise takes you beyond your limited zone of concern to imagining yourself as a citizen of the universe. You will begin with your own body and then expand outward to the community of fellow seekers.

Hidden Community

Practice deep breathing for five minutes, on the pattern of inhaling for twelve counts, holding for six, exhaling for twelve, and holding for six. During this time, picture your inner self opening to the cosmos: expectant, loving, and serene.

During the second five minutes of this meditation, think of the others around the world struggling to establish themselves in the practice of meditation just as you are. Perhaps even take one minute to think of those who are reading this book, doing these exercises just like you. Send these fellow travelers the same positive energy that you have experienced in your meditation. Wish them success in all of their material and spiritual endeavors. Picture their physical bodies healed of any health conditions, and wish them vibrant health and longevity. See their questions answered, their problems solved. Know that others are wishing the same for you, and feel this hidden support for all that you do. When the time has expired, consider reaching out to others on the path of meditation through a web posting, e-mail, or phone call.

Twenty-Minute Monotasks

In this section, you are deepening your meditation by lengthening the time period. Having an object for meditation, whether a text or something in nature, will help you to maintain your focus throughout the meditation. These exercises are the heart of this guide to meditation, and here you will discover a path of meditation that you can follow throughout your life.

Sacred Reading

Find one of the classics of the world's religions and select a chapter for reading. Consider the *Tao Te Ching*, the *Dhammapada*, the *Bhagavad Gita*, the *Ramayana*, the *Qur'an*, the *Psalms*, the *Gospels*, or some other well-known, time-honored text. Familiarize yourself with the book ahead of time and choose a chapter that "spoke" to you especially. If you underline or highlight while you read, choose a chapter that has a lot of your own personal notations. That is a good sign that there is material for you to work with. As you read the text, look for a portion that speaks to you directly. A phrase will seem to jump off the page, as though it was meant specifically for you at this moment in your life. Turn the phrase over in your mind again and again until you have it memorized.

Then shut your eyes and allow it to continue to repeat in your mind, filtering all distractions and focusing solely on the words. You may even boil the text down to a single word or image, which can become the touchstone for gathering your attention.

When you have five to ten minutes left—you'll know when—begin a quiet dialogue with yourself about the text. Ask how you can apply its insights to your life. You may find that, in a flash of inspiration, you have the answer that you have been seeking. If nothing comes to you, don't sweat it. Try again later with the same passage or a different one.

Meditating with Your Eyes Open

Find a quiet place to sit in nature. Sit still and listen. Observe your surroundings with all of your senses. It may sound strange, but try to listen even with your eyes. Wean yourself away from the need to comment internally on what you see. Put all of your energy into simply receiving what you find in that place. If concerns from the day intrude, gently let them go. Practice with intensity and cultivate a sense of expectancy, as though something amazing were about to happen. Allow the scene to become more intense and wash over you, as though you were a matchstick in a flood. Discipline your mind and do not allow it to wander. Continue this practice for twenty minutes. When you have time, increase the duration to half an hour and then to one hour.

Solar Exercise

Keep a journal for a week of your exercise, eating, and meditation habits. You don't need to get into fine details about calorie counts and workout specifics; just jot down a few notes each day. See if you can identify ways that you habitually mistreat your body and mind and find a few simple ways to make changes. Be careful not to castigate yourself. Keep it lighthearted and stick to areas where you can do better fairly easily. Repeat this exercise every few months.

Lunar Exercise

Get out a clean sheet of paper and some colored pencils and make a sketch of your body. It doesn't have to be a work of art, just pretend you are a child coloring. Note any areas where you have pain by shading in red or gray. Make note of any parts of your body that make you feel awkward or self-conscious. You can choose a color for these if you like. See if you can find the attitudes and habits that lead to your discomfort with your body. The next time you sit in meditation, retrace these causes to their sources and thereby diffuse them.

CHAPTER SUMMARY

- Meditation harnesses *prana* or *chi* (*life energy*), which can be used to create wellness.
- Chronic pain and other health conditions can be directly alleviated through the practice of meditation.
- Meditation should not be used in place of healthy lifestyle choices like good diet and exercise.
- Knowing a few simple yoga postures will help you to sit comfortably with better posture.
- This chapter increases the length of meditation to twenty minutes with two key exercises.

CHAPTER 10

FOCUSING ON THE BREATH

Breath control can help you stop your stress. Because of the way your body works, deep breathing interferes with the stress response. With practice, you can learn to stop stress before it even starts—just by paying attention to your breath.

Repairing Your Body

As a recovering multitasker, you may be learning to focus on one thing at a time, but the sheer amount of information coming at you in any given day can make it hard for you to sort out what matters, what you should care about versus what you should ignore.

Fortunately, you have a natural ally in meditation, specifically meditating with and through breathing, traditionally known as *pranayama*, breath control, or deep, slow breathing.

The billions of neurons in your body relay information at astonishing speeds, effectively connecting each part of the body to every other part. In a stressful situation, including the self-induced stress of multitasking, your brain perceives a threat, just as it would perceive a physical threat like a mugger in the parking lot or a bear in the woods. As we discussed in Chapter 1, your body immediately jumps into hyperdrive.

Over time, your stress response causes a whole host of health problems, like high blood pressure, weight gain, insomnia, digestive problems, and even diabetes. Some stress is good, but chronic stress fries the body's systems. Over time, small problems become serious ones as the wear and tear compounds.

Your body does have its own way of dealing with these problems. When you sleep, your central nervous system repairs some of the damage. Your brain is very active at certain points as you sleep, assimilating what has gone on during the day. That's where all your anxiety dreams come from. But you also have periods of dreamless sleep, which is when your body does its real rest and repair work.

In the yogic tradition, dreamless sleep is regarded as the most beneficial, and it is this state that meditation seeks to replicate. Dreaming sleep may be more interesting from a psychoanalytic or even psychic point of view (where do all those chickens come from?), but for our purposes, dreams are a distraction from repairing the damage of daily life, which is the goal of meditation.

Breath control helps your body stop some of the damage before it can even start. When you breathe slowly and deeply, you take direct control of the stress response. Your lungs send an "all's well" message to your brain, getting it to chill out and stop producing all of that adrenalin. As you breathe deeply, your heart stops beating so quickly, and your blood pressure decreases. Feelings of calm and well-being replace a sense of panic.

In meditation, you don't just breathe slowly and deeply, you concentrate on your breath, bringing all of your awareness to it. (Of course, sometimes you'll use other visualizations and of course no one can get rid of distraction completely.) The goal is single-pointed awareness, which combats the stress associated with perceived threats. Concentrating on breathing becomes a substitute object of thought, which contains the active mind. The conscious mind's nature is to be active, so it must be given a task. The simple task of watching the breath or performing a visualization moves the conscious mind away from the everyday panic-inducing visions of personal, professional, and financial ruin that absorb so much energy. By moving the mind down to a simpler level of functioning, it has time to recuperate and will stop pushing stress down the line to the body.

Choosing a Saner Way

You may be saying to yourself, "Well, that's great, but isn't it a little bit irresponsible to take refuge in watching my breath while the world goes on without me?" You may be thinking that the situations in your life cause stress because they are stressful. You may have come to expect and crave the rush of adrenaline that comes with the stress response. In fact, you may have a hard time getting anything done without it.

In order to move into a different way of doing things, a subtle shift in perspective must happen, a desire to do things in a calmer and saner way.

When you open your eyes from meditation, especially after habitual, sustained practice, the world will literally look different. You'll feel like you just got a new pair of glasses—the details will look sharper, colors brighter. Everything will seem vibrantly beautiful and alive. This won't happen all the time, but you will notice it from time to time. Because you have taken conscious control of your mind through meditation and breath control, your mental landscape has become decluttered. You can see the world better because so much junk has been removed. The problems that felt so overwhelming are now put into proper perspective. Just as an overcoat draped over a chair can seem like an intruder in your house at four in the morning, a small life event can seem like a catastrophe when your system is panicking. When you meditate, especially when you practice breath control, you will approach problems in calmer manner, and solutions will come more readily. Over time, your whole outlook will change, and the world will seem a lot less gloomy and threatening. You will feel more in charge of your own life, which will give you a natural feeling of confidence and optimism.

The Basics of Breath Control

It all begins with a breath. A short answer would be to breathe more deeply, all the time. Few of us could maintain that kind of mental discipline, though, so it's best to work the breath control into meditation and, from there, let the practice find its way into everyday life. The important thing is to learn when the breaths are long enough and how to maintain the right rhythm.

The 4/8 Count

Begin with a 4/8 count, which is to say, eight seconds inhaling, holding four seconds, eight seconds exhaling, holding four seconds. One cycle takes you twenty-four seconds, which may not sound like much, but compare that with the typical two-to-four-second cycle, and the difference is profound. Your lungs will be inflated much more fully, and you will feel the stretch in the often-tense muscles of your upper back, like getting a massage from the inside. Your chest will expand forward, leading to better posture. Don't worry too much about your stomach for now, but it will naturally rise on the inhalation and fall on the exhalation.

Beyond the 4/8 Count

When you are fully comfortable with the 4/8 count, you can move to a 6/12 count for thirty-six seconds per cycle. This will be a little more challenging, but easily manageable for most people. Occasionally you can experiment with a 10/20 count for a one-minute cycle, but you don't need to maintain this rhythm on a daily basis.

Don't Stress Over It

If you feel a sensation of panic, like you're not getting enough air, immediately shift down to a shorter breath. After all, the goal is stress reduction. Don't feel the need to prove yourself by taking longer breaths. If you work too hard at breath control, your conscious mind will become overactive and you won't get the results you seek. Give the practice enough effort so that you're working a little bit, but not so much effort that that you feel like gasping.

How to Count

In the beginning, you will need to count to yourself to maintain the rhythm. You can keep a clock nearby to listen to the ticks, or count mentally without worrying about an exact one second duration. You can also count "om one, om two, om three," as is often done in yoga classes, to remind you of the meditative purpose and slightly lengthen each count.

Once you get established in the rhythm, it's okay to let go of the numbers and just keep breathing at the same rate. You will establish a muscle memory that tells you when to stop.

At the beginning, it will take a lot of mental energy to maintain the counting, but after a few minutes, the conscious counting will recede into the background and you will be able to work on a visualization, sacred word meditation, or other technique.

The counting is beneficial at first, because it helps prevent you from thinking about other things. When you do get distracted, just gently return awareness to the breath.

Turbocharging Your Meditation

Breath control is a good way to get a boost out of meditation that would take much longer otherwise. Even if you can't get a grasp on one-pointed awareness, just doing the deeper breathing alone will produce benefits. When you get into stressful situations during the day, you can easily begin to lengthen your breath and move to a feeling of calm, which would not be possible without practicing intentional periods of breath control.

You may hear people saying, "take a deep breath," as a little piece of advice for stressful times. In this case, the conventional wisdom is true, but to get maximum benefit from deep breathing, you need to attune your body to it. Your mind and body will come to associate deep breathing with that sense of calm, and, over time, you'll experience cumulative benefits of practice. You'll reach a relaxed state more easily, eventually becoming calmer with a single deep breath. It takes work, though, to reach that point, so getting into a regular routine is very important.

As you get further into the practice over weeks and months, you may notice some other changes taking place. The most obvious one will be that it becomes easier to lengthen each breath: What seemed like an uncomfortably long breath before will now seem almost normal. As we discussed in Chapter 9, you may start to sweat during meditation or experience other feelings of heightened life energy. They show you're making progress, but don't depend on them, because they may not always come. Concentrate on doing your part and let the results fall where they may. Remember, meditation is not a competition, and each person has an individual journey, which means that what each person considers important will also vary.

One-Minute Monotasks

Here you will find some quick exercises that can be done in the midst of a busy day as well as some longer ones to increase your stamina. Work on the longer exercises in the mornings and evenings and the shorter ones throughout the day. Try each exercise at least once and return to those that you find inspiring.

One-Minute Breath Control

Practice deep breathing by inhaling for eight counts, holding for four counts, exhaling for eight counts, and holding for four counts. You will go through two cycles in just under one minute. Try doing this throughout the day whenever you have a free minute: while waiting for your computer to start, while sitting in a checkout line or at a red light. As you breathe deeply, intentionally bring yourself to a state of calm.

Sanity Break

Watch for spikes in emotion throughout the day, and pay attention to your own warning signs for overload. You may feel blood rushing to your face or a racing feeling in your chest. When this happens, stop for one minute, close your eyes, and breathe deeply. At the end of the minute, go back to whatever you were doing in a better frame of mind.

Five-Minute Breath Control

Put your feet flat on the floor or sit on the floor cross-legged or in half lotus position. Set a timer for five minutes. Pull your shoulders back and open your chest; this should give your spine a nice lumbar curve. Placing a cushion or a phone book beneath your buttocks may make the posture easier. Close your eyes and keep your head tilted downward slightly. Imagine a string pulling up through the crown of your head, and lengthen your spine.

Now begin breathing deeply. Inhale for eight seconds, hold for four seconds, exhale for eight seconds, and hold for four seconds. Keep going with this rhythm until it becomes more natural.

Once you feel like you have it, stop counting. Continue to maintain the same pattern of breathing. As stray thoughts arise, bring your awareness back to your breath, concentrating on the cycle of breath as it moves into your nose, down through your throat, and into your lungs. Continue in the same rhythm for the remainder of the time, and close with, "Om, shanti, shanti, shanti. Om, peace, peace peace."

Moving Beyond Boundaries

Sit quietly and practice deep breathing. Concentrate on feelings of universal love and gratitude. Magnify those feelings as much as possible. Do you sense any resistance on your part? Can you think of people you find it hard to love? Can you think of situations where you lose your patience, where you get angry? Can you think of times when you hold back from giving life your very best? Breathe into those problem areas and fill them with goodwill. Think of the transformation of those negative parts of life. Imagine yourself with deep reserves of tranquility, more than enough for any situation you might face. Picture yourself maintaining calm focus throughout those challenging situations, becoming more than you were yesterday, more than you are today. Give yourself permission to grow, to become greater and more at peace.

Twenty-Minute Practice

This is the standard practice that you'll eventually build to doing twice daily. As you begin your session, notice any fears that may creep into your mind. You may worry about taking time away from other priorities, or you may fear connecting with yourself through silence. Simply acknowledge the fear and leave it alone, like it's a guest in your house. Be grateful for the fear, for it shows that you are transcending your own self-imposed boundaries. Prepare yourself for greater listening and receptivity with breath work.

Establish yourself in a 6/12 rhythm. Inhale for twelve counts, hold for six, exhale for twelve counts, hold for six. You may need to count to yourself for several minutes. As soon as you can maintain the rhythm of deep breathing without the numbers, let them go. Don't worry if you are still counting despite yourself. The internal dialogue will gradually weaken as you continue with the exercise.

Begin to listen deeply with your physical ears and your inner ears. Become totally receptive. Imagine your ears getting larger and larger, like the ears of an elephant. (It's okay if the image makes you smile.) Watch any thoughts that may arise. You may not be able to stop thinking altogether, but you can slow down the chain of thoughts and put more spaces in between the thoughts. Imagine that your stream of consciousness is flowing slowly, like molasses.

Focus on making your body transparent and light. Imagine the night sky surrounding you, and let the boundary between yourself and the world grow thin. If a breeze were to blow through the room, it would go right through you. Light from the stars above shines through to the floor. You are a luminous, transparent being, radiating peaceful light.

Now enter a period of silence, or near silence. If you find yourself feeling anxious or not knowing what to do, just go back to deep breathing and watching the breath. If you still feel anxious, you may wish to say a little prayer, something like, "The kingdom of God is within me," or "I am bliss." And now, quiet listening.

Now you begin to emerge from the silence, but take the attitude of listening with you. Allow it to overflow into your daily life. Become more attentive and awake. Notice things that you wouldn't ordinarily notice. When you are ready, chant "Om, shanti" and open your eyes.

Solar Exercise

Take several readings of your heart rate and blood pressure over the course of one week. Average your findings, write them in a journal, and keep them somewhere safe over the coming months of meditation. Check the numbers again each month. Do you see verifiable results of your meditation? Allow meditation to lead you to other positive lifestyle changes, like eating well and exercising. The point of this exercise is not to collect scientific data, but to give yourself a means of seeing tangible results, which is one way to keep yourself motivated.

Lunar Exercise

The English word, *inspiration* comes from the Latin, *spirare*, breathing in. In cultural traditions around the world, life, creativity, and divinity are associated with wind and breath. Take a look at Hindu iconography of Hanuman, son of the Wind (*Vayu*), as he leaps across the ocean with a mountain of beneficent herbs to aid in the fight against the demon king, Ravana. Or look at an Orthodox Christian icon of Jesus being baptized in the River Jordan, as the holy spirit, represented as a dove, is borne on the winds to reveal to the disciples that he is, indeed, the Son of God. If you enjoy Greek mythology, look for images of Aeolus, the king of the winds and son of Poseidon, who gave Odysseus hospitality and swift passage so that he could (finally) return home. Consider collecting wind imagery or making your own wind artwork to inspire your own journey.

CHAPTER SUMMARY

- Breath control directly intervenes in the body's systems, creating a natural pathway to increased calm.
- Breath control practice should gradually increase in duration over time so as not to produce strain.
- Adjust your rate of breathing if you feel like you are not getting enough air or must strain to keep the rhythm.
- Breath control can be practiced spontaneously whenever you need to take a break, and it should also be built into morning and evening meditation sessions.

CHAPTER 11

FOCUSING ON THE MIND

Meditation can help you preserve and enhance your memory by helping you access where memories are stored and retained. Meditation can also improve your creativity and help you overcome blocks.

Meditation and Memory Loss

Memory loss can be caused by dozens of factors, ranging from the after effects of surgery or medication to diseases like Alzheimer's and Parkinson's to alcohol and drug abuse to mental health concerns like anxiety and depression.

Each cause has its own particular origin and treatment program, including medical and psychological interventions but meditation can improve the situation for you no matter why it has happened.

When it comes to preserving good memory, what is good for the heart is also good for the brain. The same diet that controls high blood pressure and cholesterol will also help the brain maintain good functioning. In the same way, the meditative techniques that slow the heart rate and lower blood pressure also lead to good brain functioning.

"The true art of memory is the art of attention."

—SAMUEL JOHNSON

Studies have shown that meditation reduces the risk of memory loss, stroke, and other disorders in old age, and also improves memory for those already over age sixty. According to a study by Sanford I. Nidich in the *Journal of Social Behavior and Personality*, the benefits cut across a wide range of mental factors, inducing "significantly higher levels of fluid reasoning, verbal intelligence, long term memory, and speed of processing."

Meditation not only improves memory in the elderly, it helps students perform well on standardized tests, executives achieve results in their jobs, and parents to remember to pick up the dry cleaning and the kids from soccer practice.

Why does meditation improve memory? The medical explanations are complex and not fully understood, but part of the explanation lies in our typical inattention as we go about our daily lives. Most of the time it's not so much that our memories are faulty as it is the case that the memory never got formed in the first place. If you have ever lost your keys, you know what I'm talking about. You set them down without paying attention to what you were doing. Your brain had no mental picture to recall when it came time to find them again.

Enhancing Creativity Through Meditation

Artists and musicians often talk of the creative experience as if it were a mystical experience. Paul Cézanne said of the process of painting, "The landscape thinks itself in me, and I am its consciousness."

"The creative person is both more primitive and more cultivated, [. . .] madder and a lot saner, than the average person."

—FRANK BARRON

We have seen in other chapters how meditation restores an overburdened mind and body, so it shouldn't be surprising that meditation gives memory and creativity a boost as well. Multitaskers make snap decisions under duress, which means that only a fraction of the multitasker's faculties are put into any given action or situation. It becomes harder for a multitasker to retain information, because the "bandwidth" of the brain is going into switching back and forth between tasks rather than fully focusing on the task at hand. Similarly, if you must act under pressure, creativity will be repressed, because the most important objective is to simply get through the task and move on to something else. Memory and creativity thrive when you are fully present to the experience, when you can contemplate how to do something *well* and not just move on to something else. Monotasking and meditation point to a qualitatively different way of responding to the world, a way of savoring each moment rather than fleeing from that moment. Time gains a certain thickness for people who make themselves available to it.

People often think of creativity as an innate quality, something you either have or you don't. But people who think they are not creative may simply not be in the habit of being creative. And many people tend to judge their own efforts too harshly. This self-deprecating attitude leaves very little room for experimentation, which is a vital part of the creative process.

Expanding creative ability requires wiggle room, space that comes from leaving well enough alone, nonjudgment, and repeated attempts. Without safe space and time, creativity simply can't get off the ground. Meditation can help you to refrain from judgment, to stop listening to the internal critic, who is never satisfied.

On the other extreme are artists, writers, and musicians who think that they are geniuses, that everything they do is simply perfect. This attitude, too, stifles creativity because it prevents further growth. If you think everything you do is already perfect, you have little reason to learn something new.

Criticism, too, has a role to play during the creative journey, because it helps sharpen skills, leading to better results. If free expression is the entrée into the creative process, taking criticism is the next threshold that must be crossed. People who can say "yes" to constructive criticism are destined to become better artists, whether or not they realize it themselves. Meditation helps in this area because it de-centers the ego and allows you to think of art that happens through you but is not necessarily by you. The meditative artist views herself as a channel for energies coming from outside the self, while the egotistical artist views art as something coming *de novo* from her own genius.

Another common problem that stifles creativity is the belief that creative work only "counts" if it reaches a mass audience. Emily Dickinson stashed her poems in baskets and drawers around her house; Melville's *Moby Dick* was considered a flop when it was first published. Would anyone consider these writers as lacking in creativity?

What reaches a mass audience today may be considered rubbish one hundred years from now, and what is obscure today may become a cultural mainstay in another generation. In fact, every new trend begins on the margins of society before the marketing machines get ahold of them. So creatives must have the courage to explore and do something new: otherwise nothing new ever gets made.

Creativity is one of the biggest factors leading to a satisfactory life. Few things are better for your mental health than digging your hands into a lump of clay or splattering some paint onto a canvas. As long as you don't depend on the acclaim of others, which may or may not come, creativity makes life more beautiful and interesting. Here are a few suggestions to get you started:

- **Hang with it.** If your creative endeavors don't look right the first time, keep going. A drawing that looks wonky at first may blossom with more time expended. Picasso often painted over his own work when he was dissatisfied. Art is about persistence as much as inspiration. Inspiration, too, takes effort: the muses communicate with those who diligently pay attention to them. Meditation allows this process of inspiration to happen, because it attunes the mind to the universe.
- **Make mistakes.** The creative process is not about the spontaneous generation of perfection but the gradual selection of beautiful aberrations. If you don't make mistakes, you don't have anywhere to begin. Perfection is paralyzing; mess is progress.
- **Show up.** Set aside some time each day for creative pursuits. Your inner self will come to trust that it has a hospitable environment in which to express itself. Think about a kid at school

without recess, a soccer mom without a cup of coffee, and you get the picture. Our creative selves need small indulgences.

- **Take breaks.** When you hit a snag, meditate, walk, dance, or sing. Come back to the table refreshed and energized. Many a revelation has occurred during the odd times, the interludes that weren't technically part of the process.

- **Expect help.** When you apply yourself with diligence to a creative pursuit, the universe colludes to help you realize it. What seemed impossible at first will become a reality as resources and collaborators appear out of nowhere.

- **Enjoy the process.** Take time to revel in the smell of paint, the texture of paper, the scratch of a pen, the feel of the dance floor beneath your feet. When it comes down to it, it's all process. Even the masterpiece is a snapshot in time, a frozen moment of creation. Creativity is a doing.

- **Detach from validation.** Keep working even if no one appreciates what you are doing. Be creative because it makes your life better, not because you expect an external reward. Praise will come with time, but don't depend on it.

- **Begin and begin again.** When you feel stagnant, do something. Blocked creativity is nothing other than the stubborn refusal to make something, write something, or sing something. Every time you get stuck, just start again. Don't make it any more complicated than that.

The meditative process described in this book greases the wheels of creativity. Meditation strengthens the architecture of your brain. You will be able to think faster, visualize better, and work steadily. Meditation also tames the voice of the internal critic. The practice at watching thoughts will translate directly into being able to suspend the voice of judgment, especially in that fragile, early stage of creativity. Meditation taps into the intuitive layers of the Self, which will create more profound expressions without conscious effort. Meditation creates intrinsic rewards, making work without validation easier to handle. You will become more self-confident, which will allow you to weather early faltering and criticism.

Meditation and creativity also complement one another by making the creative life more bearable. The histories of music, painting, and literature are rife with the stories of broken people who succumbed to mental illness and substance abuse. These tragic lives suggest that creative endeavors are not the breathless, carefree pursuits that outsiders tend to see in the arts. Oftentimes, creatives are under more pressure than people with more conventional lifestyles, because the competition for work is more fierce. Strategies for stress relief should be a part of the standard training for every artist. Meditation can bring more balance to the lives of part-time and full-time artists of all persuasions and disciplines. Meditation also reduces burnout in careers characterized by ups and downs—heights of elation and depths of despair.

Working Without Judgment

Working intuitively and banishing judgment makes the creative process much less painful and more invigorating. The Taoist term, *wu wei*, which literally means *non-action*, but might be called *active passivity*, adequately describes this experience. Athletes might call it being "in the zone": that space which is neither consciously planned nor an automatic reaction but lies somewhere between the two in a kind of meditation-in-motion. Creativity expert Mihaly

Csikszentmihalyi calls this state "flow," which he uses to describe a "process of total involvement with life" that leads to deep joy and insight.

Whatever label we attach to this state of complete immediate awareness, a few simple signs reveal when it is happening. Time seems to stand still or to advance very rapidly: several hours pass as though in a few minutes. Vast quantities of work are done seemingly without effort: the book, the play, the opera seems to "write itself." External stimuli fade into the background; distractions disappear without any conscious effort at concentration.

This state, which countless people from all walks of life have experienced, seems almost magical. If we could enter it at will, we would all be hyper-productive and creative, but perhaps the laundry and the dishes would never get done. Nature has a way of bringing us down from these highs so that the business of life can continue. When the high goes away, the hard slogging begins.

Creativity and Balance

Creativity happens in the productive tension between daily grind of work and intuitive flights of fancy. When these two forms of activity combine, the result is most powerful. Just as a battery must have two poles in order to provide current, we must all have both self-discipline and inspiration in order to be happy and productive people. Self-discipline without inspiration is a joyless, meaningless exercise, while inspiration without self-discipline is idle fantasy.

Flashes of inspiration feel wonderful, as poets, mystics, and scientists know equally well, but those bits of intuition are not meant to be filed away mentally or just jotted on the back of a napkin. No, these little brilliant gems of new thought should be conveyed to the world in the form of new inventions, new literary works, or new philosophical and religious movements. Because our futures are intertwined with those of every other living thing, we owe it to ourselves and to the world to polish our crafts, to become better at what we do, and to tell others what we have found in a way that it can be received. When we work with our whole hearts, holding nothing back, we release a powerful current into the world that changes reality itself for everyone.

The Timing of Invention

You may agree with what I've said so far but have fallen out of touch with your own muse, your tutelary spirit. Meditation can help get you back on track again by restoring balance to your life and opening the floodgates of inspiration. As you meditate throughout the day, wait for inspiration during the transition times at dawn and dusk. You will have your greatest discoveries upon rising first thing in the morning, before your conscious mind has time to extinguish the natural lucidity of the receptive state of sleep.

In the evening—in the hours just after dark—creative energies peak. When dinner is over and the dishes cleared, the kids in bed and the dog fed, steal a few precious minutes to recollect yourself and see what waits there. Don't try to force it. You may not even want to intentionally meditate. Just sit quietly with a cup of tea or some other small ritual and the ideas will come.

Pay attention also to the rhythms of the year—the changing seasons, the cycles of the moon, and the holidays associated with them in your own tradition. Just going outside each night for a minute or two to notice the moon and the stars will go a long way toward awakening creativity. Experiencing the weather—rather than just making small talk about it—will get your juices flowing. Taking a walk outside is the best cure for any sort of mental blockage. Don't fix your routine rigidly, but allow it to bend with the seasons. Go to bed a little earlier in the winter and a little later in the summer. Allow yourself to join with the world outside. Let the powers of nature blend into your own efforts.

When you feel blocked, like things just aren't working with your project, step back and meditate or do routine work that does not require branching into new directions. Concentrating on the small stuff—filling in the background on a painting, adding some footnotes to a book project, cleaning the studio or workspace— will allow you to zoom forward when the moment comes. Don't depend too strongly on grace or on effort alone, but allow the two to commingle throughout the creative process.

The Power of Will

It is almost impossible to overstress the importance of developing a powerful will. Almost all modern meditation teachers stress this in one form or another. Obstacles do exist, but none of them have permanence; their apparent solidity is an illusion. If you do not believe that anything can stand in your way, nothing will.

Start from the premise that anything that might block your full creative expression can be overcome, and solutions will begin to appear. You will need a very strong power of belief in order to succeed in creative endeavors, where competition is often fierce and success can be a long time coming. You will have to begin and begin again, over and over, oftentimes without much encouragement. But if you believe in the higher Self that works through you, time will be on your side. Those small efforts will begin to snowball into an unstoppable force, and those inspirations will find a public voice.

Over the years you will run into many people whose dreams have stalled, who have consciously or unconsciously decided to stop creating, to stop progressing in their spiritual paths. The excuses that these people proffer are myriad—financial or health problems figuring prominently—but one thing they have in common is that they believe their problems are intractable, that their issues in life are insurmountable. This belief in the insurmountability of obstacles is the toxic faith that poisons all efforts, the one sure way to failure. Hardly anyone would admit to deliberately failing, but such defeatist attitudes are self-inflicted wounds meant to sabotage the creative self. Don't try to "fix" people who believe there is no solution to their problems; until they can admit at least the possibility of change, all of your words will fall on deaf ears.

Above all, do not discuss your own struggles with creative types who choose to remain stuck. You risk falling into a negative feedback loop that will suck the life out of your efforts. Keep conversation with such people as light as possible, and notice their tendency to accentuate the negative. Your caring self will feel bad at times when holding people at arm's length, but remember, the best way that you can be of help to faltering creatives is to succeed in your own endeavors.

Perhaps your own recovery into the freedom of the creative life will serve as some inspiration to those around you who seem to have lost their resolve. When one person breaks out of negative habits and embraces good ones, it creates a wave effect that empowers others to do the same. Whether you know it or not, other people are watching you all the time, taking cues from your behavior and deciding how to live based on your example. None of us get to opt out of being a role model for others. The only question is to decide what kind of a model we will be. The younger generation and your peers are counting on you to be the very best person that you can be. It is well worth the effort to realize that greatest Self. Not only will you be happier, you will also be contributing to building a better world, a world which desperately needs your insights, your own unique vision.

Get started today at writing that short story, finishing your degree, dusting off those painting supplies, picking up that instrument, or whatever else you have put on hold until a more opportune time. The opportunities come to those who make efforts on their own behalf: today is the opportune time. This does not mean picking yourself up by the proverbial bootstraps, it just means getting started. Make something, build something, or do something to express your dream in concrete form. Otherwise your dream will remain just a dream forever. *Tempus fugit, memento mori.* Time flies, remember that you will die. This ancient saying has great wisdom to it. In remembering our own brief span of life, we accelerate our greatest priorities in the face of death. Death teaches us to truly live. Regardless of your age, you must think about the legacy that you would like to leave behind. Life is too precious to waste in despair. Hope feeds on our best efforts.

Five-Minute Monotasks

The following exercises will help you to see how the creative life fits into the life of meditation. You will move deeper into your storehouses of memory to find new inspiration and realize your dependence on the cosmos.

The Möbius Strip

Take a strip of paper, twist it halfway, and then tape the ends together to form a Möbius strip. Trace your index finger along any surface of the strip and you will see that it returns to the starting point but on the "other side" of the paper. If you go around again, you will arrive at the exact same point. Mathematically, the strip only has one side even though it appears to have two. The Möbius strip models the relationship between your "internal" thoughts and the "external" world. Upon close investigation, you will see that the world flows through you as you move through the world. The mind and the body, the inside and the outside, are not strict opposites but two parts of the same reality. Keeping this paradoxical image in mind will help you to understand how meditation alters your reality.

A Teaspoon of Soil

Hold in your hand a teaspoonful of soil. Look at all of the small particles you can see with your eyes: grains of sand, decaying bits of leaf, dark humus. Maybe you have managed to scoop up an ant or some other small insect. Realize that beyond what your eyes can see are millions of bacteria, nematodes, and other micro-organisms. In this teaspoonful of soil is the basis for life, the foundation for the food chains that make up ecosystems. Close your eyes and appreciate the dense web of relationships upon which all life depends. Think about the earth itself as a living organism and realize your place in its functioning.

Ten-Minute Monotask: Hidden Refuge, Hidden Mentors

Practice breathing deeply on an 4/8 rhythm: breathe in for eight seconds, hold for four seconds, exhale eight seconds, hold four seconds. Continue with counted breathing for three to five minutes or until you can hold the same pattern without much conscious effort.

Think of a place where you felt safe as a child: a favorite place in the woods, a tree for climbing, or your grandmother's kitchen table. See yourself in that place and make your vision as detailed as possible, just as if you were there in person.

You may wish to imagine a guide or mentor there with you: the spirit of someone who has passed away, a guru or teacher, or a saint or savior. When you are sufficiently established in the visualization, you may wish to have a conversation with that guide, asking questions about major decisions and turning points in your life.

Use this exercise any time you need comfort and guidance, but never undertake it in a frivolous manner. While it might help you to find some lost car keys, its power is better used for creative and spiritual growth. When the exercise is going well, you may wish to extend it for twenty minutes or even longer. Jot down some notes when you are finished, and make sure to act as quickly as possible on any advice that you receive.

Solar Exercise

Test your memory by dealing five playing cards, looking at them for thirty seconds, and putting them face down. See how many of the cards you get right. Try again after meditating and see if your concentration improves. Chart your progress over time, and gradually increase the difficulty level. If you see no progress over a few weeks, you might consider taking herbal or vitamin-based memory supplements. If you can't get a majority of the cards right, you may need to see a medical doctor.

Lunar Exercise

Do you have a muse, someone you imagine in conversation while working on creative projects? An old creative writing professor? A hero or mentor? Your grandmother? A sage or goddess figure? Maybe it's more of a place that gets you going: a park where you played as a child or a city like Chicago or New York. Paint a picture of your muse and hang it in your work space. It will keep you going when your creativity seems to ebb.

CHAPTER SUMMARY

- Younger and older adults can benefit from the memory-enhancing powers of meditation.
- Meditation improves the speed of information-processing, enhances verbal memory, and strengthens reasoning ability.
- Meditation enhances creativity by cutting through judgmental thought processes.
- Meditation leads to greater freedom and spontaneity in creative pursuits by keeping you in the moment.

CONCLUSION: MEDITATION AND THE UNEXPECTED

One cool fall morning at my brother's place, I grabbed my cup of coffee and started walking up the mountain behind his house in Northeast Georgia. The property bordered on the National Forest, and old logging skid paths laced their way through the mixed hardwood forest. I hoped to go up the mountain and find a quiet place to sit for a while.

I walked along the PVC pipe that carried water to my brother's house from a small spring up the slope. Then I cut up past the swaths of rhododendron and mountain laurel, an increasingly rare sight due to development in the hills. I don't know if I really found the summit, because the landscape confused me for a while. I wasn't walking on a trail exactly, because the old skid roads could end abruptly, requiring some improvisation.

So I found a log on the shoulder of the mountain and sat down with my cup of coffee. I took a few deep breaths and began to relax. I hadn't been there five minutes when I heard the sound of crunching leaves behind me. I assumed that white tail deer were tromping through the woods, a common enough occurrence, and paid the sound very little attention. I went back to my morning contemplation without giving it much notice. As the sound grew closer, however, I could no longer ignore it. I stood and turned around.

There about eight feet from me were two black bears, a mother and a juvenile. The mother had a look of surprise on her face, and, for a second, our eyes met. That one second held an eternity as we mutually recognized one another, wondering what to do next. The bear and her cub, not exactly a cub but perhaps a teenager, turned to the right and trundled into the underbrush, and the chance meeting was over.

It lasted only a few seconds, but I will never forget that day.

I went back down the mountain with a lighthearted feeling, like I had been elected in some way to see those bears. It was what one of my teachers, Brian Mahan, would have called an "epiphany of recruitment." That event would be partially responsible for my later academic work on animals, in which I tried to find ways of thinking about the deep-seated respect that humans should have for other creatures. I felt such an absence of fear up there on the mountain, but instead just a kind of awe at coming face to face with a creature that perhaps could have harmed me but showed no desire to do so. I wanted to return the favor in some way, to get people to respect bears and other animals more.

I tell this story to demonstrate that unexpected things happen when you deliberately go into a mode of stillness and listening. The world will begin to open in surprising ways: everything will be suffused with radiance, a hidden energy at the heart of reality. The staid, quotidian way of objectifying the world will give way to a new vision in which the world erupts onto the scene of consciousness. The experiences of mystics through the ages are not just meant to fill the pages of dusty tomes in libraries—they are practical guides to what can happen when you open your mind and life to reality.

We might call it a *higher* reality, but it would be better to call it a *deeper* reality. The experience of the world as mundane is triggered by a kind of blindness stemming from inattention. Shopping malls and offices are filled with the walking dead, and I'm not talking about zombie movies. When we experience an external reality as filled with inert things, life naturally doesn't seem particularly interesting. When we desire to be affected by the world, when we no longer see the world as inert, it comes to life. When you go out to meditate, have conversations with your surroundings. Say to the trees and to the sky, "Show me your hidden dimensions. Show me who you really are." You will feel quite insane, but, when you say this with every fiber of your being, amazing things begin to happen.

The old dividing lines of external and internal, living and inanimate, will fall away for a brief time, giving a glimpse of what religious people call *heaven*. That word is so loaded as to almost become meaningless: it conjures up images of angels playing harps on clouds and probably also ideas of punishment and reward from the old man in the sky. *Heaven* is nothing other than being wholly and completely immersed in the present moment. It is that time-standing-still feeling when all distractions, *all* distractions disappear and the world appears in its true glory. It is an attunement stemming from mental and physical discipline, the results of the labor of attention.

I am trying hard not to speak in metaphors, but permit me just one. If you wear glasses, you know that dust accumulates on the lenses, so that your vision is covered with a thin film. You don't notice these specks in your field of vision because they are so close to your eyes. You just gradually get used to them. Finally there are so many specks that you finally wipe them off on your shirt tail. It's amazing how much difference this makes. Suddenly the world becomes more clear, and you can see the sharpness of detail you couldn't see before.

This is what meditation (or prayer or contemplation, if you would prefer) does for your mental life—you clear away the debris that keeps you from truly experiencing reality. When you have moments of peace, moments of bliss or mystical vision, it's not that reality has changed. You have just cleared your field of vision so that you can see things as they really are.

The world is a beautiful, magical, or divine place (choose your adjective), but most of the time we walk around looking at our shoes, thinking about bills that need to be paid and things that need to be done.

The most tragic part of living in this dreary state of mind is that it kills time: minutes, hours, days, weeks, months, and years pass without enjoyment.

Our lives are made of time, and killing time is killing ourselves. So we have to make the most of the time we have been granted, striving always to see the energetic reality that surrounds us. If you continue in the practice of meditation, you will experience the kinds of things I have been describing, and perhaps you already have.

Other "paranormal" things (called *siddhis*, powers or perfections, in the yogic tradition) will also begin to happen. You will receive hints out of nowhere about how to tackle problems, you will see things that haven't happened yet, and you will intuit exactly what other people are thinking. The reason I put *paranormal* in quotes is that these experiences are normal, it's our crazy lives that are abnormal. When you meditate, you return to the natural insight or intuition that is the birthright of every human being.

A Few Cautionary Remarks

When these odd occurrences happen, avoid the temptation to make them the point of your practice. When you make spiritual experiences the point of meditation, you subtly veer off course. The point is not to have cool experiences; taking drugs can accomplish that. The point is rather to come home to yourself. The point is to stop wandering into fantasies of the future and memories of the past and just be *here* for awhile. At the same time, if you don't have these experiences, do not take it as a yardstick of how things are going. When you meditate and feel like you are getting no results, you are undergoing a subtle recalibration that will one day produce fruits.

With practice, you will be able to tell when to give yourself slack with meditation and when to buckle down. If you sense that you are on the cusp of a breakthrough, by all means hold on to your attention with everything that you have. Keep going until that sense of higher awareness washes over you. At other times, and you will know when—perhaps when you are completely exhausted or experiencing a major upset—you will want to slow down a little bit. Some meditation can help get you through tough times, but it is probably not a good idea to push yourself hard during these periods.

Keep in mind that you are in it for the long haul. You may at some point want to drop everything and just meditate. This will, indeed, produce results, which you might see as further encouragement. Unless you can basically live a monastic lifestyle, though, this kind of continuous spiritual exercise cannot be sustained. If you neglect other duties, you will eventually burn out and have to give up meditation altogether for a while. It is better to practice a little bit less and be able to meditate for decades than it is to meditate twelve hours a day and only be able to sustain it for a few months. You have to keep your personal and professional life going while you meditate so that the path remains clear.

You should also find spiritual sustenance in taking care of yourself. You will find all sorts of books that recommend ascetic practices like fasting and avoiding sleep. These techniques do work, but they are dangerous and should only be practiced for short periods of time under the watchful eye of a trained spiritual director. Otherwise you could end up with insomnia or anorexia, which could be worse than if you never meditated in the first place. If you are practicing by yourself, it is best to get plenty of food and sleep and make sure to keep up your personal hygiene and professional appearance.

One other caution is to avoid feeling superior to other people. You may think that this goes without saying, but as you begin to make progress, you may wonder why everyone doesn't meditate. As your head swells, your heart will close, and a subtle sense of judgment will slip into your thoughts about those who have no form of spiritual cultivation. This superior attitude is toxic and will kill any gains that you have made.

Even worse, it is hard to remove once it creeps into your mind. If you start feeling this way about others, it is time to change tactics. Go eat some ice cream, watch a movie, take a nap, or do something that you consider particularly unspiritual (though not unethical). Then go out of your way to understand and appreciate the point of view of the person that you have judged. After you take a break for a few days, resolve to continue your practice with greater humility and humor.

Above all, do not try to convert anyone else to the practice of meditation unless they have already expressed an interest in it. More likely than not, your efforts will backfire and the person will think less of the spiritual practice than they did before. The best way that you can share with others is to perfect your own life as much as possible: be kind, loving, patient, and happy, and others will want to discover your secret. Use discretion even when someone asks you to tell them what you are doing. At this stage in your practice, you are very fragile, and criticism or ridicule could be very damaging. If you have to live or work in atmospheres that are hostile to spirituality, you may even have to practice in secret. Know that many people around the world have had to do the same thing, and sometimes they have become great saints.

Remember, also, that technique is a means to an end and not the end itself. Sometimes people can get so fixated on technique that they forget the internal realities that the technique seeks to instill. You should listen to your yoga teacher when she gives you an adjustment, but don't get so obsessed with the proper form that you are afraid to do it wrong or afraid to go to class in the first place.

Similarly, when repeating prayers or mantras, don't be so concerned with the exact wording or pronunciation that you forget the intent behind the words. If some spiritual practice feels too complicated to you, feel free to simplify it or ignore it altogether. It may not suit your lifestyle at this time, and that has to be okay sometimes. We can't all be monks and nuns, and this book is intended to make meditation accessible to even the busiest executive.

The same thing goes for the exercises in this book: if something doesn't work for you, change it. Feel free to go at your own pace. If a few things from this book jump out at you as particularly worthwhile, by all means keep doing what works. Meditation should empower people and should not feel like a straitjacket. Spirituality is always a choose-your-own adventure, no matter what anyone might say. So give yourself a little latitude. Let yourself explore world traditions, read about the science of meditation, and take a look at religious artwork. You may find yourself wandering in a direction you never expected, and that is all part of the journey.

Closing Thoughts

You have now begun a practice that you can continue for the rest of your life. You will have a hidden refuge of deep calm available to you anytime you need it. You will find aspects of yourself you never knew were there, unlock hidden talents and find deep intuition. You will come closer to the mystery at the heart of the universe and discover deeper connections with others. You will foster improved mental and physical health and have greater memory and creativity. The practice of meditation can be just the sort of boost you need to bring you greater satisfaction in life.

Where you go from here is up to you. You can keep going with the practices in this book indefinitely; they are open-ended enough to yield benefits at all levels of practice. You may stumble onto a new spiritual tradition or return to the tradition of your childhood. Or you may see meditation in an entirely secular light, as a way to enhance performance. No matter where this path leads, walk it in confidence, knowing that millions have gone before you.

Eventually you may find yourself to be the leader in any room where you are present. Others will notice your calm in the face of difficult situations, and they will begin to look up to you. People will wonder where you gain such great composure. Use your abilities for good: to help other people, to advance worthwhile causes, to look out for those at the bottom of organizational hierarchies. You will be able to see things that others can't see: the subtle aspects of a situation available to someone who truly pays attention. When everyone else is afraid and confused, you will be a noticeable presence, a refuge of strength in difficult times.

If one commodity is in short supply these days, it is careful attention. The more complicated our lives become, the less we can attend to any part of life with the consideration needed. You meditate not only for yourself but for the world. When you refuse to live an insane life, when you live with simple wisdom gained from within, you make the impossible possible. You empower others to also live productive, peaceful lives. You help to reverse the ever-present culture of fear and anxiety that surrounds you every day. In short, you become peace and love for the world.

That may sound like a lofty goal, but it is attainable for you. Just think of the strides that you have made while reading this book. The days ahead hold greater possibility than you have previously imagined, and you yourself hold more potential than ever before. Awaken to that potential, and you will change the world. I hope that this book has been of service to you, and I always love to hear from readers. Go away from these pages knowing that you hold the keys to your own destiny, that your own heart is the heart of the universe. Aum shanti.

APPENDIX

FOR FURTHER READING

Chapter 1

Bregman, Peter. "How (and Why) to Stop Multitasking." *Harvard Business Review* Blog. May 10, 2010.

Fendrick, A. Mark, Arnold S. Monto, Brian Nightengale, and Matthew Sarnes. "The Economic Burden of Non-Influenza-Related Viral Respiratory Tract Infection in the United States." *Archives of Internal Medicine 163*, No. 4 (Feb. 24, 2003): 487–494.

Hellgren, J. Cervin A., et al. "Allergic Rhinitis and the Common Cold—High Cost to Society." Allergy 65, No. 6 (Nov. 26, 2010): 776—783.

Hamilton, Jon. "Think You're Multitasking? Think Again." October 2, 2008. National Public Radio.

Ihnatko, Andy. "Multitasking Is a Lie—Your Brain Needs a Break." *Chicago Sun-Times*. September 26, 2010.

"'Infomania' Worse than Marijuana." April 22, 2005. BBC News.

Micucci, Dana. "Meditation Helps Some Students." *International Herald Tribune*. February 15, 2005.

Naish, John. "Is Multitasking Bad for Your Brain? Experts Reveal the Hidden Perils of Juggling Too Many Jobs." UK *Daily Mail*. August 11, 2009.

Ophir, Eyal, Clifford Nass, and Anthony D. Wagner. "Cognitive Control in Media Multitaskers." PNAS August 24, 2009.

Rosen, Christine. "The Myth of Multitasking." *The New Atlantis: A Journal of Technology and Society*. Spring 2008.

Toto, Christian. "Transcending Stress; Doctors Back Meditators' Claims of Calm, Health Benefits." *Washington Times*. December 9, 2003.

Chapter 2

Dillard-Wright, David and Ravinder Jerath. *The Everything® Guide to Meditation and Healthy Living*. Avon, MA: Adams Media, 2010.

Mahan, Brian J. *Forgetting Ourselves on Purpose: Vocation and the Ethics of Ambition*. San Francisco: Jossey-Bass, 2002.

Chapter 3

Halifax, Joan. *Being with Dying: Cultivating Compassion and Fearlessness in the Presence of Death*. Boston: Shambhala, 2009.

Medina, John. *Brain Rules: 12 Principles for Surviving and Thriving at Work, Home, and School*. Seattle: Pear Press, 2009.

Chapter 4

Kynes, Sandra. "Appendix A: A History of Altars." In *Your Altar: Creating a Sacred Space for Prayer and Meditation.* Woodbury, MN: Llewellyn, 2007.

Kingston, Karen. *Creating Sacred Space with Feng Shui: Learn the Art of Space Clearing and Bring New Energy into Your Life.* New York: Three Rivers Press, 1997.

Linn, Denise. *Sacred Space: Clearing and Enhancing the Energy of Your Home.* New York: Random House, 1995.

Streep, Peg. *Spiritual Gardening: Creating Sacred Space Outdoors.* Makawao, HI: Inner Ocean Publishing, 2003.

Chapter 5

O'Hara, Kathleen. *A Grief Like No Other: Surviving the Violent Death of Someone You Love.* New York: Marlowe, 2006.

Chapter 6

Allen, David. *Making it All Work: Winning at the Game of Work and the Business of Life.* New York: Penguin, 2008.

Cameron, Julia. *The Right to Write: An Invitation and Initiation into the Writing Life.* New York: Tarcher, 1998.

Chapter 7

Subramuniyaswami, Sivaya. *Dancing with Śiva*. Kauai: Himalayan Academy, 1997.

Yogananda, Paramahansa. *The Law of Success: Using the Power of Spirit to Create Health, Prosperity, and Happiness*. Los Angeles: Self-Realization Fellowship, 1989.

Chapter 8

Johari, Harish. *Chakras: Energy Centers of Transformation*. Rochester, VT: Destiny Books, 1987.

Matt, Daniel C. *The Essential Kabbalah*. New York: Harper, 1998.

Nouwen, Henri J.M.. *The Wounded Healer*. New York: Doubleday, 1979.

"What Is Hinduism?: Modern Adventures into a Profound Global Faith." *Hinduism Today*. Kapaa, HI: Himalayan Academy, 2007.

Young, Louisa. *The Book of the Heart*. New York: Doubleday, 2003.

Chapter 9

Sivananda Yoga Vedanta International. *www.sivananda.org*. Includes overviews of yoga philosophy, pranayama, and asanas (postures).

Yoga Journal. *www.yogajournal.com*. Includes helpful illustrations of the asanas described in the chapter.

Chapter 10

Dillard-Wright, David and Ravinder Jerath. *The Everything® Guide to Meditation and Healthy Living*. Avon, MA: Adams Media, 2010. (See Appendix B for selected list of medical articles and links.)

Jerath, Ravinder. *www.mindbodyresponse.com.* See Dr. Jerath's very helpful articles and multimedia presentations.

Chapter 11

Chambers, Richard, et al. "The Impact of Intensive Mindfulness Training on Attentional Control, Cognitive Style, and Affect." *Cognitive Therapy and Research, 32* No. 3 (2008): 303–322.

Csikszentmihalyi, Mihaly. *Flow: The Psychology of Optimal Experience*. New York: Harper, 1990.

Nidich, Sanford I., et al. "Effect of the Transcendental Meditation Program on Intellectual Development in Community-Dwelling Older Adults." *Journal of Social Behavior and Personality 17*, no. 1 (2005): 217–226.

Thompson, Barbara, et al. "What is Healthy Aging?" *Generations 25*, No. 4 (Winter 2001–2002): 49–53.

INDEX

N

ABOUT THE AUTHOR

David Dillard-Wright teaches philosophy, religion, and ethics at the University of South Carolina Aiken. His other works include *Ark of the Possible: The Animal World in Merleau-Ponty*, an exploration of animal behavior and cognition as related to the works of the French philosopher. His previous book with Adams Media, coauthored by Ravinder Jerath, is titled *The Everything® Guide to Meditation and Healthy Living*.

David has also published articles and reviews in academic journals as well as encyclopedia entries on animals and ethics. He speaks at conferences throughout the United States and Canada and gives retreats and workshops related to his writing. He lives in Augusta, Georgia, with his wife, Jessica, his sons, Atticus and Oscar, and his dog, Pearl.

CD CONTENTS

1. Morning Reflection [1:32]
2. A Taoist Meditation Break [1:25]
3. One Minute Anxiety Tamer [1:19]
4. Just Breathe [1:54]
5. Living in Gratitude [1:44]
6. Vanquishing the Task Monster [5:40]
7. Releasing Negative Thoughts and Emotions [6:06]
8. Five-Minute Tune-Up [4:55]
9. Dealing with Distraction [10:02]
10. Ten-Minute Standard Practice [10:54]
11. Twenty-Minute Standard Practice [20:09]

Narration by Jim Infantino at Notable Productions.
Vibes compositions written and performed by Dan Cantor at Notable Productions. Copyright © 2011, MayCan Music.
Harp compositions written and performed by Lorena Perez at Notable Productions.